W9-AFV-337

PRAISE FOR

BEYOND THE FINAL SCORE

As a faithful FCA teammate for more than 50 years, Coach Osborne has traveled across the country challenging thousands of coaches and athletes to realize there is more to life than winning ball games. *Beyond the Final Score* is a must-read for all ages, especially if you want to get fired up about making a difference in the world.

DAN BRITTON

Senior Vice President of Ministry Advancement, Fellowship of Christian Athletes

I met Tom Osborne for the first time in 1980 when Florida State flew into Lincoln, Nebraska, to play the Cornhuskers. I was in the Seminole locker room, and there was a knock on our door. I opened it, and there stood Tom Osborne. We shook hands and Tom said, "Is everything okay? Do you need anything?" I had never had an opposing football coach come by before a game to see if we were okay. Never had one since, either . . . but this is Tom Osborne. If you are an aspiring young coach and want a role model to follow, be sure to read *Beyond the Final Score.* Tom did it the right way, and though he suffered some along the way, he always finished on top. What makes a man great is his ability to recover and fight back, and this book will show you how to do it.

BOBBY BOWDEN

Head Football Coach, Florida State University

When most people think of Tom Osborne, they think of a great football coach. When I think of Tom Osborne, I think of a man of character who quietly but effectively improves the lives of everyone he encounters.

WARREN BUFFETT

Investor, Businessman and Philanthropist

Celebrity is only important in how you use it—whether you use it to help people or not. Tom did that. He could have endorsed a football shoe or something and made more money, but he chose to do something with his celebrity that would make a difference in the lives of people.

ERIN DUNCAN

Legislative Director for Congressman Tom Osborne

Beyond the Final Score reveals Tom Osborne's key not only to success but also to one's satisfaction with the "final score." I got to know Tom when I was Speaker of the House and Tom was elected as a congressman from Nebraska. He wasn't the flamboyant person you might expect a nationally renowned coach to be. As a congressman, he had a quiet nature but was focused and very tough when it came to negotiating the things he saw as important to him and the folks in Nebraska. In this book, Tom lets us see how that man of solid values and vision came to be.

SPEAKER DENNIS HASTERT
Former U.S. Congressman and Speaker of the House

Tom Osborne's character, consistency and integrity have always caused me to hold him in high esteem. He recruited me out of high school, and though I did not attend the University of Nebraska, I rooted for them from a distance solely on the basis of the respect I had for their leader. Not only did his players benefit from his example, but I did as well.

PASTOR NAPOLEON KAUFMAN
Former NFL Running Back
Senior Pastor, The Well Christian Community Church

Tom Osborne is an All-American hero in my book! His humility and commitment to serving others is what separates him from so many others. I've seen it demonstrated firsthand on the athletic field and in the U.S. Congress. His words still serve to inspire and motivate me!

STEVE LARGENT
Professional Athlete and Member of Congress

Victory without honor is an unseasoned dish. It might fill you up, but it won't taste good. I have long admired how Tom Osborne has stood tall in so many arenas, winning with integrity, a humble spirit and honor.

JOE PATERNO
Head Football Coach, Pennsylvania State University

Football is such a great game. It teaches so much, and it is truly hard to just step away from it. For Tom Osborne and for myself, our relationship with the players was the best part of coaching and something we carried beyond the game. When it comes right down to it, Tom not only knows how to win football games but also how to win in life.

GRANT TEAFF
Former Head Football Coach, Baylor University
Member, College Football Hall of Fame
Executive Director, American Football Coaches Association

Coach Osborne has been one of the most profound role models in my personal and professional life. He is the man we all would hope to be, the coach that we aspire to be, and the selfless leader that has made our nation so great. Our coaches and players will gain a great deal from this terrific book!

JIM TRESSEL
Head Football Coach, Ohio State University

I have great respect for the legendary Tom Osborne. What a life! And, now, what a book! *Beyond the Final Score* will impact you deeply, as it did me.

PAT WILLIAMS
Senior Vice President, Orlando Magic
Author, *What Are You Living For?*

Tom Osborne is one of the finest people I have ever met. He obviously was a great football coach, but he is more than that. He was a dedicated public servant and always did what was right. His character is unimpeachable.

FRANK WOLF
Congressman, Tenth District of Virginia

Tom Osborne has always gone beyond the final score, achieving competitive greatness with integrity, hard work, selfless service to others and a strong faith.

JOHN WOODEN
Former Head Basketball Coach, UCLA and Member of the Basketball Hall of Fame

TOM
OSBORNE

BEYOND THE FINAL SCORE

There's More to Life Than the Game

Regal

From Gospel Light
Ventura, California, U.S.A.

Published by Regal
From Gospel Light
Ventura, California, U.S.A.
www.regalbooks.com
Printed in the U.S.A.

Library of Congress Cataloging-in-Publication Data
Osborne, Tom, 1937-
Beyond the final score : there's more to life than the game / Tom Osborne.
p. cm.
ISBN 978-0-8307-5111-2 (hard cover)
1. Christian men—Religious life. 2. Osborne, Tom, 1937- I. Title.
BV4528.2.O83 2009
277.3′082092—dc22
[B]
2009022746

3 4 5 6 7 8 9 10 / 15 14 13 12 11 10 09

Dedicated to my wife, Nancy. She has enabled me to take on myriad roles and has been a remarkable model of living each day with a servant's heart.

CONTENTS

TAKING ON MY NEXT ROLE

Twenty years from now you will be more disappointed by the things you didn't do than by the ones you did do. So throw off the bowlines. Sail away from the safe harbor. Catch the trade winds in your sails. Explore. Dream. Discover.

MARK TWAIN

Never Say "Never"

Just when you think that you know how the rest of your life will play out . . .

After 25 years as head football coach of the University of Nebraska Cornhuskers, I knew it was time to move on. There were still things I wanted to do with my life—and, before long, I would be fortunate enough to accomplish many of them—but I believed my days in Nebraska athletics were over.

In 1997, when I turned the football program over to my successor, Frank Solich, I was ready for my next role. I ran for the U.S. Congress and won. I ran for governor of Nebraska and lost. My wife, Nancy, and I started a mentoring program called TeamMates. I taught graduate classes and spent more time with my family, but I also stayed busy speaking at events and writing a book. I even went fishing.

But just when I thought I knew how the rest of my life would play out, I got a call.

A decade after retiring as head coach, I was asked to return. Nebraska's football program was experiencing difficulty. In 2004, the team's losses had outnumbered its wins—and a losing record was nearly unfathomable in Lincoln. The 2005 and 2006 teams had winning seasons; however, they lost four games in 2005 and five in 2006. During the 2007 season, the team was teetering on the brink. After a 3-0 start, the Cornhuskers lost to USC, Missouri and Oklahoma State. At that point the athletic director was fired (although the win-loss record was not a major factor in the decision), and the team went on to lose four of the next five games, resulting in its second losing season in four years. When the athletic director position came open, I was asked to step in on an interim basis.

Certain positions bring notoriety, even celebrity. I have never been completely comfortable with either, and I knew that taking the job would be news—as athletic director, I would be under the watchful eyes of reporters, boosters, fans and Internet bloggers (I am glad that there were not too many bloggers when I was head coach!). Returning to the scrutiny of the public eye was not entirely appealing, yet at the same time, I didn't think that a desire to avoid publicity was a very good reason to turn down the position.

I prayed, talked with my family and mulled over the pros and cons of the proposition. When I was confident that I had reached the right decision, I rolled up my sleeves and got to work. There was no fanfare. When I left 10 years before, I never contemplated coming full circle. Yet in a paradoxical way, my intervening ventures into politics, the classroom and the nonprofit world—and all I learned from those experiences—prepared me for what I would face in my new job.

I *was* back, but in a new role with very different challenges.

Sometimes when I walk into Memorial Stadium, I recall a particular game we won or a play that turned a game around. I cherish those moments and think fondly of the players and coaches who accompanied me on that part of my life's journey. Books have been written about that era, by me and by others. Nothing will ever replace or duplicate the national championships, the strategy sessions, the practices, the fans or "taking a knee" in prayer before each game. Being a coach at Nebraska, which I have written about in my previous books, *More Than Winning*, *On Solid Ground* and *Faith in the Game*, gave me a chance to experience all that, and much more besides.

But "coach" was neither my last nor my most important role.

As each of us takes our journey through life, we move in and out of various roles. Some of these are common to most people: child, student, neighbor, spouse, parent, coworker, friend. As teens and then as adults, we take on more specific roles: musician, stockbroker, rancher, chef, counselor, nurse, and so on. I have been blessed to take on a wide variety of roles in my lifetime. I have been a professional athlete, a coach, a congressman, a teacher and an administrator. I have been a leader in various capacities, a public figure, a father and a husband—and a fisherman.

It is my hope that, through it all, I have been God's servant.

This book is a collection of my observations about life, character and spiritual significance, and of reflections on the lessons I have learned in the many roles I have played. It is my hope that, as I tell these stories, you will be inspired to think about the roles *you* play and how you measure success in each one.

Saying Yes

In the 2008 film *Yes Man*, Carl Allen (played by funnyman Jim Carrey) discovers firsthand the heady joy of Cornhuskers football. On a spontaneous trip to Lincoln, Nebraska, Carl and his girlfriend, Allison, join the teaming, screaming "Sea of Red" in Memorial Stadium and experience for themselves what hundreds of thousands of Huskers fans look forward to every September: the thrill of the game.

At the beginning of the movie, Carl isn't doing much with his life. He's unenthusiastic about his job as a loan officer at a local bank. He sits at home every night, watching TV and avoiding calls from his few remaining friends. His ability to reach out to others and invest in meaningful relationships is nearly paralyzed. In short, he is afraid to say yes.

But before too long, Carl has an experience that transforms him from a person overcome by fear to a person who joyfully embraces whatever life brings his way. He has no way of knowing that he won't be hurt by his next experience or relationship—and, in fact, he discovers that pain is almost guaranteed—but finding the courage to say yes turns out to be the key that unlocks Carl's sense of purpose and meaning for his life . . . and that brings him to a Cornhuskers game!

As I look back on my own life so far, I see many turning points. Some of them were obvious at the time, but others proved to be major crossroads only in hindsight. Often, I didn't see God's hand at work until much later, even though I tried to seek His guidance along the way.

It's sometimes difficult to feel confident that we are making the right decisions and going in the right direction. Years ago, I was torn between two careers: coaching or university administration. The idea of heading a college or university was very appealing, and I earned my graduate degrees with that end in mind. But I also had an enduring love for the game of football, and when the door opened to a life spent on the field and in the locker room, I said yes.

But the decision to say yes took about a year. Back and forth I went, between education and football. My wife, Nancy, and I talked, and I prayed about it. The truth is that life as a football coach did not make as much sense, at least on paper, as that of a college teacher or administrator. Teaching is a much more secure and stable career, while coaching usually entails moving every three or four years and competing with other ambitious coaches for a very small pool of positions. There are only a small number of people who ever get the opportunity to be a head coach for a major program—how could I even dream that I could be one of those select few?

Coaching also often takes a toll on family. Many marriages simply can't take the stress. I can't tell you the divorce rate among coaches, but I have a number of colleagues who are on their second or third marriages. As I considered a career in coaching, I weighed how my decision would affect my marriage and my family. Could I be a dedicated husband and father *and* be a good coach? When Nancy agreed to marry me in 1962, she knew that I was a graduate assistant football coach, but she assumed that I was headed toward a career in academia. Was football coaching going to be fair to her?

The wonderful 2006 movie *Facing the Giants* tells the story of a high school football coach whose marriage is crumbling and whose team is falling apart. Between the demands of coaching and the demands of being a husband, Coach Grant Taylor is pulled in too many directions to make anything he does work very well. The problem is that he has his priorities all wrong. However, through a series of painful events, Coach Taylor learns a lesson that I was fortunate to learn early on: The only sure way to make a marriage *and* a coaching career thrive is to say yes to serving God. Even when we make mistakes—which is inevitable—God can use them to shape us into people of character who make the most of the roles that He has planned for us.

Coaching was not the safe choice, but it proved to be a decision that would challenge me in ways I never imagined. By saying yes to a life in a highly competitive arena, I was saying yes to a life of learning to balance the roles of "coach," "husband," "father," "friend" and many others.

With the End in Mind

Is success just about winning? Acclaim? Trophies? Wealth? Our personal happiness or satisfaction? I have been blessed to experience some of these over the years, and I can answer without batting an eye: No. Accomplishments, applause, awards and fortune are rewards that often come as a result of hard work and a determined spirit, but there is something bigger. Something better. Something that will outlast the winningest season, the plushest corner office, the heftiest bonus and the loudest cheers. That something can only be found when we look beyond the final score.

Bob Devaney, the head coach of the Nebraska Cornhuskers football team from 1962 to 1972, and the man who helped to launch my coaching career, understood this well. When I last went to see him, I knew that Bob was dying. His family had made the difficult decision to remove him from life support, and I wanted to see him while he was still lucid enough to know that I was there.

As I sat by the bedside of this larger-than-life friend who had been a presence in my life and career for so many years, I couldn't help but reflect on the nature of success. Bob's wife and his children had gathered around to share with him and each other whatever time he had left. He'd had a stroke, which made it very difficult for him to speak, but he wouldn't let a little thing like a stroke stop him. He knew he didn't have much time left, and he wanted to make sure the people who were most important to him knew that he loved them.

When he could choke out a few words, Bob didn't talk about being named NCAA Coach of the Year in 1971. He didn't talk about the national championships Nebraska had won during his tenure as athletic director. He didn't mention the money he had made over the decades of his successful career. What mattered to Bob at the end were his family and friends—the relationships that made him who he was.

Even though Bob was not known to be a religious man, he nodded his head when I asked if I could say a prayer for him. A tear rolled down his cheek as I finished, and I knew that the prayer had been significant to him. At the end, relationships, family and spiritual matters are often the only things that count.

I've had the privilege to have been with a number of people at or near the end of their lives, and something I've never heard even one of them say is, "I wish I'd spent less time with my family" or, "I really should have focused on making more money" or, "If only I had worked longer hours!" Sadly, I *have* heard people near the end of their lives express a wish to go back and do things differently, to focus on what is actually important rather than chasing after things that cannot last.

On a Mission

I've been a long-time admirer and avid reader of Stephen R. Covey, founder of the Covey Leadership Center (now FranklinCovey®) and author of *The Seven Habits of Highly Effective People*. In this perennially bestselling book, Covey argues that to live a truly effective life, we must align ourselves with "true north" principles that will develop in us a strong character.

Character is very important to the book's premise. Covey writes about the process of researching the book and discovering that, in the literature written in the first 150 years of our nation's history, success is inseparable from strong character. A successful person was honest, generous, self-sacrificing and trustworthy. By contrast, in much of the literature written during the past 70 years, success is more about *perception:* influence, charisma, possessions and recognition. One of Covey's goals in writing *Seven Habits* was to reorient our concept of success toward character, rather than personality.

One of the "true north" principles that can develop strong character is *begin with the end in mind.* Many people wander their way through life, one appointment to the next, without thinking very deeply about their purpose or intentions. In response to this tendency, Covey recommends an interesting exercise: writing your own eulogy, including what you would want a family member, a business associate or a friend to say about you. The focus of a eulogy is to remember and celebrate the character of the deceased, to highlight the kind of life he or she lived.

It's not difficult to see how such an exercise can help us dig down to the bedrock of what life is about. At my funeral, I'd like someone to say, in complete honesty, "Tom tried to serve and honor God. He was a person who did his best to live out his faith. He was not a phony. He did what he said he would do; he was consistent and his word was good." Whether or not someone will say it, I don't know. But I want to live in such a way that these comments are not too hard to imagine.

Please bear in mind that I am very human and have many failings. I can only hope that the general trajectory of my life has been pleasing to God. I recently read an article in the *Chicago Tribune* that said that about half of former Protestants and Catholics who were now unaffiliated say they lost their faith because they view religious people as "hypocritical, judgmental or insincere." Sadly, many of us do not live out the faith we profess very well. Also, people of faith are often held to an almost impossible standard by many of those who observe them.

After writing the eulogy, Covey next recommends composing a personal mission statement that is consistent with the core values outlined in the eulogy. We can think of a personal mission statement like a personal Constitution, guiding the decisions we make to keep us on the right course, much as the U.S. Constitution guides our government to stay on the course set for us by the founding fathers. A mission statement can help us live with intention and purpose, prioritizing and focusing our attention, energy and passion on what is most important to us. As we drift off course, the mission statement keeps pulling us back to our core values and a life of purpose.

The process of writing a personal mission statement requires a good deal of reflection, because you are working backward from the things that you want someone to say about you to the kind of values and principles that you need to live by in order for those things to be true of your life. Articulating these core values is the heart of the matter; knowing and understanding your purpose—what gets you up in the morning and what brings you peace at night—is key to living an effective, fulfilled and truly successful life.

My personal mission statement is *serve and honor God in all things*. Sounds pious, maybe a little too religious for some. However, as I stood on the sideline and watched a player fumble as we were about to put a game away, as an official's call turned a possible national championship into another loss, as I disciplined players and my own children, as I did my income taxes, what other mission statement could call me back to "true north"? What line in the sand could help me examine my actions in light of what God would have me do other than seeking what would honor Him? Living by this mission statement doesn't mean that I always got it right, but it does mean that I've always had a standard by which to measure everything I did—a standard that does not depend on my mood, on what others think or on what is expedient. With time and practice, imperfect as I am, I have gotten better at implementing the mission statement.

One thing about my mission statement: It doesn't allow me to play games. I might fool others, or even fool myself, but God looks on the heart, and I have never figured out a way to fool Him.

Full of Purpose

Three thousand years ago, the Greeks noted that balance was very important in living a successful life. They noted that an educated person was one who had grown in all three dimensions of human experience: physical, mental, and spiritual. Most people who are familiar with ancient Greek culture recognize that the Greeks did believe in physical fitness. They started what is now known as the Olympic Games, and emphasized physical conditioning and athletic competition.

I am somewhat concerned because at present, in the United States, we are less active as a nation than we once were, and this particularly applies to our young people. Instead of participating in various types of games and athletic contests, we now have a great many young people spending hours every day in front of a computer, playing video games, on cell phones, texting or just listening to music. As a result, childhood obesity has become a great problem and Type II Diabetes, which is directly related to being overweight, has become a major health epidemic among our young people.

Some young people are quite active in athletics, however; instead of playing pick-up games after school they are channeled into swim clubs, Little League baseball teams, midget football teams and other organized sports that are fairly specialized, even at the early ages of seven, eight, or nine. The result is that for many children, physical activity has lost its spontaneity. They don't get the chance to experience the sheer enjoyment of playing a game of kick the can, touch football, basketball or any of the pick-up sports that many of us older folks experienced during our childhood years.

The Greeks recognized that part of a balanced life—and part of one's education—would have a strong intellectual element as well. Students of history will recognize that the Greeks were the most advanced civilization of their time and had outstanding philosophers, poets, mathematicians and other intellectual giants who were often ahead of their time. Again, I have some concerns about the amount of time our young people devote to playing electronic games and other time-consuming activities that are not always very intellectually challenging. Sometimes I wonder if our children are spending enough time reading—particularly reading books of substance that can lead not only to intellectual growth but also to character development.

A third dimension that the Greeks felt was so important in creating balance in a person's life was the spiritual dimension. We often hear speakers talk about how to be successful, or we read books on self-improvement and success, and spirituality is rarely mentioned. I find it interesting that when people enter an athletic arena where they realize they are going to be stretched to their full capacity and possibly beyond, often they have an impulse to tap into a spiritual resource that might carry them through. When people are about to go into battle, one often finds that spirituality becomes fairly significant in the preparation process. Someone once said, "There are no atheists in foxholes."

I'm sure that there are some atheists in foxholes; however, a great majority of those who are in great danger are quite apt to turn to God for help in a time of crisis.

And so, the Greeks said that a truly educated person was one who has done his or her best to develop physically, intellectually and spiritually. In our culture, we tend to think of education dealing only with the intellect, but I have come to believe that the Greeks had a point, that education is multi-faceted and requires us to develop all that we have. At Nebraska, we certainly place a great deal of emphasis on developing our football players physically in the weight room and on the practice field, yet we also place a heavy emphasis on academic performance and intellectual acuity. You can't play major college football and be without intellect—the playbook is invariably quite complex.

I have also come to believe that spiritual preparation is every bit as important as physical and intellectual preparation in regard to top performance. We often use the term "spiritual," but what does it mean? According to the dictionary, "spiritual" is that which has to do with the spirit, not with those things that are tangible or material. It has to do with the soul and often relates to God. Anyone who has seen athletics up close realizes that an athlete's whole heart and soul must be involved to reach peak performance. That's why I consider spiritual preparation just as important as physical and mental preparation.

Through my years as a coach, I came to believe that a strong spiritual nucleus on a football team—or in any organization—is very important. It doesn't mean that those in leadership proselytize or attempt to coerce people into beliefs they do not hold, but that they give people an opportunity to develop their spiritual side along with their physical and intellectual side.

Each year when I was coaching football, we had an average of six to nine players drafted into the National Football League. These players had what might be called the "American Dream." They had money from signing with an NFL team, they had celebrity from being successful football players, and they had talent and youth. Our culture, and especially those in the advertising business, would have had us believe that these young men, at age 22 or 23, had everything they would need to be totally fulfilled and happy for the rest of their lives. And yet, I often saw these young men leaving professional football as somewhat broken and disillusioned individuals.

I began to puzzle as to what might have happened to cause them to move from such a promising life to one of discouragement and despair. As I reflected on it, I realized that many of these players were mostly one-dimensional. They had developed their physical abilities—they knew how to block and tackle, they had been champions in the weight room—and yet when football was over and the blocking and tackling ended, there was nothing in their lives to give them any purpose or significance.

The majority of our players had college degrees, so you would think that they would have been fully functioning, healthy individuals when their playing careers ended. However, this often was not the case. Many of these young men had been recognized and honored for being great athletes since the time they were young, and when the cheering stopped and they no longer could claim the identity of an athlete, it was often devastating for them and led to a loss of purpose, significance and meaning.

In contrast, there was always a group of individuals who seemed not to be as affected by the vicissitudes of athletics, by being cut from the team, or by having their career ended due to injury. These were people who had not only developed their physical skills and their intellectual abilities but had also developed a strong spiritual base. They realized that they'd been given the gifts of athletic ability, of fame, of a certain degree of fortune, and of youth, and they had decided to honor God with what they had been given rather than serve and honor themselves. It seemed that this spiritual stance made all the difference, as individuals who were spiritually grounded seemed able to weather the slings and arrows that go with termination of a career at a very young age and suddenly having to strike out in an entirely different direction. They seemed to have balance in their lives and were able to negotiate the difficult landscape they had to traverse.

Having such a nucleus of spiritually committed players and coaches made a significant difference on our football teams toward the latter part of my coaching career. These people tended to be quite team-oriented and were not caught up in turf battles, self-aggrandizement or selfish behavior. They were tremendously helpful in creating the kind of team chemistry that enables everyone to pull together in one direction.

I've found in my personal life that practicing the spiritual disciplines of prayer, scripture reading, and meditation have been very powerful in terms of my own preparation for whatever life might hold.

The great reformer Martin Luther is said to have remarked, "I generally pray two hours every day, except on very busy days. On those days, I pray three." Luther was a busy man—translating the Bible into German, defending his theology, writing books and leading the Reformation—so I imagine the majority of his days were three-hour prayer days! Most of us cannot claim to be that busy, yet we fill our days chasing after short-term goals, running from meeting to meeting and from activity to activity, and rarely stop to prayerfully consider how what we are doing in the present will affect our long-term mission. Our relationships with God, family and friends get overshadowed by the busyness of life.

I have found that if I want to live purposefully and focused on my mission, it is important to practice spiritual disciplines of prayer, meditation, Scripture study and worship. I could never claim to be the spiritual giant Martin Luther was, but his general principle rings true in my life: The more difficult and pressing the task at hand, the more time I need to spend with spiritual disciplines. To use the weight room vernacular, we often want to be 400-pound bench pressers spiritually but only go into the weight room on Christmas and Easter—this doesn't work in strength training, and it doesn't work in creating spiritual strength, either.

As I cultivate the spiritual, intellectual and physical dimensions of my life, the more I am able to live out my mission statement. At the end of my life, I want to know that I did all I could to achieve that purpose, because being a servant who honors God is the role of a lifetime.

Three Choices

When adversity strikes—and it will—I think we have three choices. The first is to quit. The second is to blame someone else. The third is to learn from the experience.

Abraham Lincoln is one of the most admired figures in history, and the success of his presidency is legendary even today. But some people don't know that long before he became president and fought to preserve the Union and end slavery, his life was stricken by one adversity after another. His family was impoverished when he was a child; they lost their homestead and had to live on public land. His mother died when he was nine. When he was a young man, his fiancée also passed away, and he went into a deep depression—he was bedridden with grief for the better part of two years. He could not afford to attend law school. He lost his first political campaign and many more after that.

It's hard for me to imagine what would have happened to our nation if Lincoln had thrown up his hands and quit in the face of so much hardship, or if he had spent his life blaming the many people who failed him instead of finding a way to succeed. He seems to have learned something from those early heartaches, and I believe they made him a better president. Rather than letting circumstances determine his course, Abraham Lincoln was proactive in moving toward what he wanted to accomplish. When he could not go to law school, he taught himself and was admitted to the Illinois state bar. Recalling his father's talent for telling stories, he practiced the arts of voice inflection and rhetoric until he gained a reputation as a formidable courtroom attorney and, later, a famous orator. He suffered many defeats in running for public office, yet he seemed to learn and grow with each defeat and eventually become, perhaps, our greatest president.

Losing and Winning Proactively

Athletic coaches face the same three choices: quit, blame or learn.

Losing occasionally is inevitable, even if your last loss was so long ago that you don't even remember it. I often remind Nebraska's current coaches and players of 1996. We'd won 26 straight games and two national championships and, to tell you the truth, many players had started to doubt that we would ever lose again.

And then we went to Arizona State. The final score was 19-0. Arizona State had 19. We had the 0.

Coming back to Lincoln, you might have thought someone had died. All the talk was about how the dynasty was over, how my coaching was ineffective, and so on. It's ironic: One would think that after having won so many games in a row we might have been given a break, but just the opposite was true. The more we won, the more we were expected to win.

Any time you have a program that has been highly successful for a long period of time, people get used to winning. (They never get used to losing.) One of the difficult things about a successful program is that it's easy to be painted into a corner. If you won 10 games last season, then 10 wins this season is not good enough. And if you win 11 games, you're expected to go undefeated. And then, once you've had a couple of undefeated seasons, losing one game is a very big deal. Two losses make it a very bad year.

That kind of unrealistic expectation can make coaching and playing in a program with a long tradition of winning very stressful. And with that kind of stress, it's tempting to forget to see each and every game as an opportunity to learn something and then run with it. It can be overwhelming to never really have an "off-season," when no one is thinking or talking about football.

I think that's part of the stress our coaches and players have experienced during the last several years. Some people seemed to think that once we had a new coach, we'd break out of the gate with a 12-win season. It isn't that easy. Once a program slips, it takes time and effort to get it back on track.

It would have been easy, after our loss to Arizona State in '96, for the players and coaches to point fingers at each other or to give up on the possibility of having a great season. But we chose option 3. On Monday afternoon, we all got together and agreed that Saturday's stinging loss to Arizona State was the best thing that could happen to us. Now our weaknesses were exposed. Now we knew what we had to work on in order to be a great team. We shifted our focus from the loss to what the loss could teach us. And what we learned resulted in nine straight wins and a trip to the Big Twelve championship game. Unfortunately, we lost that game to Texas, but had we won it, we would have played for a national championship five straight years.

I like to remind Nebraska's current teams about that year. I also tell them that things are never as bad as they seem when they lose, and they are never as good as they seem when they win. The final score is only one measure of well-played football; even when they win, there are still things to learn. Every Monday morning is a new opportunity to ask, "What can we take away from Saturday's game that will make us better? Where do we go from here?" The key is to be proactive, whether we win or lose. People who adopt a reactive stance toward adversity usually quit, give up easily or blame someone else for their failures. Seldom are they very effective. Those who see opportunity in difficulty and hardship, on the other hand, usually do much better with their lives.

On a Mission Together

At Nebraska, like most places, people like to win. They like to win football games, and also like to win in all other sports. But our mission is not to win. The mission of the University of Nebraska athletics department is to "serve our student-athletes, coaches, staff and fans by displaying *integrity* in every decision and action; building and maintaining *trust* with others; giving *respect* to each person we encounter; pursuing unity of purpose through *teamwork*; and maintaining *loyalty* to student-athletes, coworkers, fans and the University of Nebraska."[1] It might be disconcerting for many fans to hear that our mission is not to win but rather to live out certain core values that, if properly followed, will lead to effective performance. But as John Wooden, the former UCLA basketball coach, points out, emphasizing the process rather than the final score is the key to maximizing performance.

When I came back to the athletic department in 2007, I could tell that something was not right. Some people were ready to quit. Some people had quit already. The first meeting I attended my first day on the job involved two mental health professionals who were offering ideas on stress management to members of the administrative staff. I could sense that there were serious stress and morale issues and that this was more than a casual exercise.

One of my first initiatives as the athletic director was to get everyone together—all 240 members of the department—to develop a mission statement. Just as I believe that a personal mission statement can be a powerful tool for making personal decisions according to one's values, so I believe a corporate or team mission statement can bring people together to achieve a common purpose.

I began by asking each person to name core values or principles that they felt were foundational to our department's success. Through a democratic process of elimination, we settled on the five core values of Nebraska's athletic program: integrity, trust, respect, teamwork and loyalty. These values would become the core of our mission.

Once we had a common purpose, a mission that nearly all wanted to fulfill, I met with each division in the athletics department to brainstorm ways that our common values and mission could be incorporated into their particular area of operation. How could the security people build and maintain *trust*? How could the food-service workers pursue unity of purpose through *teamwork*? How could the medical staff give *respect* to each person they encountered? How could each sports' coaching staff display *integrity* in every decision and action? How could my specific area, administration, maintain *loyalty* to student-athletes, coworkers, fans and the university?

I also did a lot of listening. It was important to me that each person in the department was given a chance to be heard, and that each person knew that he or she was valued. Out of that long process, I think that healing began to occur. And a healed, whole body and a purposeful spirit are important things to have if we want to complete our mission.

Our mission, as a department, is to "*serve* our student-athletes, coaches, staff and fans," and I hope we take our role as servants very seriously. This servant mindset means that we put others before ourselves, to give preference to the needs of others over our own. It is my hope that as we in the athletics department at the University of Nebraska practice the art of service within our programs, the spirit of servanthood will spill over into the many other areas of our lives. A habit of serving is cultivated over a lifetime, but it can be developed in each and every role we are called to play.

Note

1. Nebraska Athletic Department Mission Statement at Huskers.com. http://www.huskers.com/SportSelect.dbml?DB_OEM_ID=100&KEY=&SPID=41&SPSID=3046 (accessed April 2009).

DEVELOPING CHARACTER

Be more concerned with your character than your reputation, because your character is what you really are, while your reputation is merely what others think you are.

John Wooden

Worldview and Character

Many years ago, I read Luke 9:24, and that verse has been instrumental in my spiritual walk ever since. It says, "Whoever wants to save his life will lose it, but whoever loses his life for me will save it." It made me think about all the ways I had been trying to save my life.

One of the primary ways that I had tried to save my life was through sports, mostly on account of my dad. Right after the attack on Pearl Harbor, my father joined the army to fight in World War II. He was old enough that he didn't have to go, but he was very patriotic. I was nearly five years old when he left, and I didn't see him again until I was almost 10.

I was very proud of my dad when he came home, but I didn't really know him. He wasn't a real person to me; he was someone who wrote a letter once in awhile, had fought in the Battle of the Bulge, and had sent my brother and me a German rifle, helmet, bayonet and even a military-style BB gun used to train the Hitler youth. But I *wanted* to know him, and it didn't take long for me to discover that sports was important to my dad and that maybe this was the way to get to know him and gain his approval. So I threw myself into football, baseball, basketball and track. If there were tryouts, I was there.

When I started playing sports, "saving my life" was the last thing on my mind. I just wanted my dad to be proud of me. But as the years passed, I gave more and more of my time, energy and devotion to excelling on the field, at the plate or under the basket. By the time I began to think about Jesus' words in the Gospel of Luke, sports had become my unconscious "sure bet" for salvation. If I played well and people approved of me, then I could feel good about myself—kind of neurotic, but that was pretty much how it was. Eventually, the second half of the verse began to make sense: If I wanted my life to be saved, I must lose it for Jesus' sake. I wasn't exactly sure what this might mean, but I figured it began with trying to put Him ahead of everything else in my life—including sports.

I haven't always succeeded. It has been too easy to let other things consume me. Even after I was done playing pro ball, I threw myself into my graduate studies, first earning a master's degree and then a Ph.D. In hindsight, my studies consumed me far more than they should have. Then I became an assistant football coach. I decided that becoming a head coach would make my life more significant and secure. I even set a deadline: age 35. I thought that if I wasn't a head coach by age 35, I would be too old, so I would go back to an academic life. You might say that I was going to try to save my life by becoming a head coach.

Bob Devaney decided to step down as head coach after the 1972 season. In his last four seasons, his teams had gone 9-2, 12-0-1, 13-0 and 9-2-1 and had won two national championships, so the bar was set very, very high. I knew that we would have to win a lot of games to stay employed. That pressure to win, at times, made winning football games another way I tried to save my life. Then I ran for public office, and winning elections fought for the top spot on my priority list.

Keeping my priorities in order has been a lifelong struggle for me. But along the way, my public decisions and personal choices have been deeply influenced by a particular view of the world. I believe that a person's character is greatly influenced by his or her understanding of how things are connected. I know that in my own situation, the way I view creation and the order of things has had a major impact on how I see everything else. So before I dive into some of the lessons I have learned about character and integrity, I want to write a little about worldviews.

How I Began to See

To some degree, the worldview a person adopts is shaped by his experiences growing up. Parents, family, neighborhood, community, culture—all these early influences make an impression on a person's life and affect his perception of the world around him. A person may choose, later in life, to reject the worldview with which he was raised, but these early experiences make an indelible impression.

It was no different for me. I grew up in a Christian home. My grandfather was a Presbyterian minister, and our family went to church and to Sunday School quite regularly. At the same time, I was heavily invested in sports and was very competitive. I wasn't sure how to square my love of an aggressive sport like football with Jesus' teachings about turning the other cheek and being humble. Although I didn't lie awake at night, troubled and sleepless because of this apparent conflict, I was bothered by and confused about how these two loves could coexist. I wasn't sure I could commit to the Christian life, as I understood it, and be a competitive athlete.

In 1957, when I was 19 years old, I went to a Fellowship of Christian Athletes (FCA) camp in Estes Park, Colorado. FCA was still in its infancy, having been founded three years before by basketball coach Don McClanen. It wasn't even close to the international ministry that it is today. The camp I attended was just the second such camp sponsored by the organization—the first had been held the year before, in 1956. Back then, the camps were targeted mostly toward college athletes, whereas today, FCA ministers largely to junior-high and high-school students.

So, the summer between my sophomore and junior years of college, I drove on my own from Hastings to Estes Park to attend the FCA camp. I'm not sure what attracted me, but I knew that it was important for me to be there.

There were a number of football players there from the University of Oklahoma, a great football program at that time. One of them was Clendon Thomas, an all-American half-back, and he was the leader of my assigned "huddle group." I had admired Clendon even before the camp, and his leadership during that week made an impact on me that lasted for many years. Oklahoma coach Bud Wilkinson, Louisiana State coach Paul Dietzel, and several pro athletes were speakers during the sessions. Bob Richards (a two-time Olympic gold medal pole vaulter), Doak Walker, Don Meredith, Donn Moomaw (great football players) and many other outstanding athletes were also there.

That week, I heard Christianity articulated by these men in a way that began to bring coherence to the internal struggle I'd been having with myself for years. I saw a vitality—a virility, even—in the Christian life that I had never seen before. The folks in my church back home sometimes seemed to me to be bland and unexcited; bored by the "wallpaper religion" that was often more of a cultural requirement than a spiritual passion.

I wanted the kind of vitality in my spiritual life I saw in the athletes around me, so I made a commitment that week to be a follower of Jesus. Although I had grown up with a primarily Christian worldview, at some point, I had to decide how I would see the world. It wasn't enough for me to thoughtlessly inherit my parents' or my community's or my Midwestern culture's view of the world. I needed to choose for myself.

I have seen the world this way for more than 50 years and have never considered turning away from the commitment I made that week, though I haven't always lived up to it the way I have wanted. I see my Christian journey like this: That week at FCA camp so long ago, I joined the team. I got my uniform, but I had a lot of practicing to do before I could be considered an effective player. Just like any serious competitor, I've had good and bad days—and good and bad plays—but I have always sought to improve my walk. Hopefully, I am a better player today than that week back in 1957 when I first joined the team.

Ways of Seeing the World

When I was coaching, we began each season by gathering our coaching staff to write our coaching philosophy for that season. What principles would we adhere to in dealing with players, staff members and each other? What values would we model to our athletes? We also collectively wrote our offensive and defensive philosophies. Were we attacking or reading the defense? Did we emphasize the run or the pass?

A mental picture of what our program should look like preceded playing the games. In a similar way, a worldview precedes how we live our lives. The theistic worldview I adopted at the age of 19 sees the world as the creation of a good Creator, designed with laws that govern both the natural and the moral spheres. But not everyone views the world in this way.

Polytheism (sometimes called animism or spiritism) was once the most prevalent worldview among humankind. People with a polytheistic understanding of the world see the activity of spirits in natural events and objects. These spirits can be helpful or harmful, according to their whimsy, and humans must try to please and appease the spirits with various prayers, sacrifices or other ritual activities. These rituals are usually performed under the guidance of a shaman or medicine man who is believed to have a unique connection to the realm of the spirits. While polytheism is not prevalent in our culture, it is still somewhat common in developing societies. Polytheists often see the world as an accident waiting to happen, where events are largely out of their control.

Naturalism is a worldview that understands the world in purely natural terms. Atheists and agnostics, most of whom subscribe to naturalism, resist the notion of a Creator. In their view, the physical universe is all there is. Humankind evolved solely by natural means, not under the guidance of an intelligent Designer who has a purpose and plan for humanity. Eventually, perhaps after many millions of years, the universe will peter out. There is no afterlife. There are certainly no moral absolutes, only personal preferences. Naturalists see the world as an accident of nature, devoid of spiritual meaning. Nature is the only god there is.

Pantheism, which is quite common in the East but has become more and more prevalent in the West through various New Age philosophies, maintains that everyone and everything is God. Everything in the physical realm is a manifestation of God; consequently, the spiritual realm is the only reality. The purpose of life is to internalize the truth of the oneness of all things, to rise above deceptive distinctions such as "good" and "evil," for these do not actually exist—both are of one substance with everything else. Pantheists see the world as an illusion to be transcended, a realm of suffering and distraction that lures away our attention from enlightenment.

Postmodernism is the most recent worldview to arise in the West. This understanding of the world basically says that man is the measure of all things, including truth. "Whatever is true for you" could be the slogan for postmodernism. God may or may not exist, but there is no way for us to know with any certainty because we are each limited by our own personal experiences and perceptions. Accordingly, we cannot know what is ultimately "right" or "wrong," only what *seems* right or wrong to each of us individually. There are no moral absolutes, except the high premiums placed on tolerance, suspension of judgment, pluralism and political correctness. To offend someone else's point of view is the one unforgivable sin. Of course, it is important to respect different races, cultures and religions and treat others with dignity and respect. However, the postmodern worldview holds these virtues almost to the exclusion of all others.

We see this worldview at work in our government, in the business world and in the athletic community. Because there are no absolutes on which people can hang their hats—the Ten Commandments, the teachings of Jesus, the writings of Mohammed in the Qur'an, postmodernism often leads to a rudderless existence with no meaningful guidelines. Postmodernists have no consistent way to measure the goodness or harmfulness of their actions. We hear people justify all kinds of misdeeds with the words, "I did what felt right," whether they are defending corruption in public office, corporate fraud or cheating on the playing field. (Most of the time, what they mean is, "I did what felt *good,*" or, "I did what was best for me.")

As a member of Congress, I had the opportunity to participate in a number of different hearings. When the Education and the Workforce Committee conducted hearings on the effect of corporate misconduct on employee retirement accounts, I was struck by the testimony of retirees who had lost everything in their retirement accounts due to CEO dishonesty. Enron's Jeff Skilling is an example. Skilling knew that Enron's books had been cooked and that a reckoning was in the offing some day soon, but he sent emails to employees encouraging them to invest in Enron stock for their 401(k) plans. He knew that the stock was all but worthless, and he wanted to sell before the bottom dropped out. Skilling made a profit from the sale of his Enron stock to his employees, while those hundreds or thousands of workers were left with nearly nothing when the scandal came to light.

This might seem like an extreme example, but I believe that Skilling's actions are symptomatic of the postmodern worldview. What he was doing was illegal, but it wasn't "wrong" from a postmodern viewpoint. In a world with no moral absolutes, right and wrong are easily blurred. *Feeling* is the only moral compass, according to this worldview. Postmodernists see the world as whatever their hearts tell them it is, and it doesn't matter if one view conflicts with another—all worldviews are equally true. I see postmodernism as standing in direct opposition to monotheism . . . but there I go rendering a judgment—the unforgivable sin.

The Christian Worldview

Judaism, Christianity and Islam, as you probably know, are the world's three major monotheistic religions. Even though these religions have at times been engaged in conflict, all three trace their origins to Abraham, Isaac and Jacob. Although they obviously do not agree on everything, they share several key beliefs: There is one God, a distinct Being who created all there is and who is active in the universe; humanity is unique in all of creation, made in God's image; the universe had a beginning and will have an end, and the course of history has a purpose; good and evil are real, and our choices between the two matter.

I am a Christian because I believe all these things, but also because I believe that Jesus was and is God's fullest revelation of Himself to humankind. Jesus' life, death and resurrection, I believe, reconciled humanity to God and can reconcile us to each other. A Christian's worldview is monotheistic, like a Jew's or a Muslim's, but is also shaped by the life of Jesus. A Christian seeks to see the world and live in the world according to Christ's example.

This doesn't mean that Christians always get it right. The apostle Paul, who wrote most of the letters collected in the New Testament, expressed his frustration that he often failed to do the right thing. In his letter to the church in Rome, he wrote:

> For I have the desire to do what is good, but I cannot carry it out. For what I do is not the good I want to do; no, the evil I do not want to do—this I keep on doing (Rom. 7:18-19).

Paul recognized that, left on his own, he could not choose to do right every single time. Through God's grace, however, which the apostle received as a free gift, Paul began the life-long process of learning to see and live in the world like Jesus.

I'm no apostle Paul, but I'm on a similar journey. I often fall short of what I should be. You might even say that I have some prodigal son in me.

Jesus told this story that is recorded in the Gospel of Luke, a parable that is familiar to many people (see Luke 11:15-32). He told of a wealthy father who had two sons. The younger son asks to be given his half of the father's estate—which, if you think about it, is akin to wishing his father were dead. The father grants his ungrateful son's request, and the son leaves home with his ill-gotten gains. He spends all the money on "wild living," the Scriptures say, and soon he's broke.

The son has no choice but to get a job, and the only work he can find is slopping pigs. He makes so little doing this dirty work that he doesn't even make enough to buy food. In desperation, he picks through the pigs' slop for edible scraps. In that moment, horrified by his self-inflicted misery, Jesus says that the son "comes to his senses." How on earth did he fall this far? Why is he stealing garbage from pigs when his father's hired hands eat three square meals a day?

So the son decides to go home and beg his father to hire him. After what he's done, the son knows that he'll never regain his favored position and the comfort he enjoyed as the son of a wealthy man—but being a day laborer is better than starving! Then a curious thing happens: The son is trudging along the road home, rehearsing his apology, when the father sees him at a distance and runs to meet him. Before the son can get two words in edgewise, the father embraces him, puts a robe over the son's tattered clothes and shouts to the servants to prepare a feast of celebration. "My son was lost, but now he is found!" he says.

Jesus wanted His listeners to understand that this is how God sees us: as His treasured children, who only have to come home to experience His loving embrace. This is a much different view of what God is like than what we see in many faiths, where God is depicted as a distant, often judgmental figure whose good graces must be earned by sacrifices, rituals and required disciplines. I have admiration for the steady discipline of practicing Islam and for the tradition and adherence to the Law of Judaism, but what seems to set Christianity apart is the concept of unmerited acceptance or grace. I coached many fine young men over the years, but there were a few who seemed utterly determined to do whatever they could to make a mess of their lives. They cultivated bad habits and focused on all the wrong things, and it was obvious to anyone watching that they were headed straight off a cliff, even if they couldn't see it.

I couldn't help but see these young men as prodigals who needed the right word or example at the right time in their lives to bring them to their senses and start them down the road toward home. It was always rewarding to see some of these players respond, do a 180-degree turn and literally become different people. This change always seemed to occur when they experienced the realization that they were loved and accepted just as they were, warts and all. They realized that there is a way we are meant to live, aligned with good instead of evil, and that realization transformed them from the inside out.

As I survey the cultural landscape in the West, and particularly here in the United States, I see a clash between secularism and Christianity. I think that we are seeing a tug-of-war between these competing worldviews. On one side, there are people who see a clear difference between right and wrong. They believe that in order for a society to function fairly and justly, the difference between good and evil must be acknowledged. On the other side, there are people who see right and wrong as personal preferences that should be left up to an individual's personal feelings. However, in drawing this distinction, it is important to point out that a rigid, judgmental, condemning form of Christianity can be very hurtful and very "un-Christian." Unfortunately, this type of Christianity is what many people think of when they consider the Christian faith, much as many think of Islamic extremism when they examine Islam.

How Things Have Changed

I think we see the effects of this tug-of-war at work in today's athletes, coaches and sports programs. A person's view of the world tells a lot about what kind of person he will be on and off the field. If he trusts a moral authority that transcends his own feelings, he will usually make decisions based on that worldview and live his life according to those higher principles. But if he trusts in his feelings as the final moral authority, he usually will not lead a life of integrity and will make decisions only on the basis of furthering his own self-interest. The same is true in business, politics and family life.

I've seen a number of changes in the moral climate of this nation since I first arrived at Nebraska as a graduate student in 1962. Back then, before coach Bob Devaney arrived, there were often empty seats in the stands, which could hold about 35,000 people. With Devaney's arrival, however, the modern era of Cornhuskers football was born—an era defined by many more wins than losses, several national championships, a remarkable number of outstanding teams and an unbroken streak of sellout crowds in a stadium that now seats more than 85,000. Although the standard Devaney established for football excellence at Nebraska has been proudly carried forward into the new millennium, things have changed.

By 1962, I had spent three years in the National Football League. Unfortunately (it seemed at the time), I had a hamstring injury that wasn't getting better, so I decided to get out of football and go back to graduate school. I arrived in Lincoln just as Bob Devaney came from the University of Wyoming to become the new football coach.

I talked with Bob about the possibility of becoming a graduate assistant coach. He said that he didn't need any coaches, but that there were some players living in the Selleck Quadrangle who had become something of a law unto themselves and were causing problems. The dorm counselors were apparently afraid to deal with them—would I like to move in and ride herd on the guys? If I agreed, he'd let me have free meals at the training table.

It was a little rough at times, but eventually the players in the dorm and I got along pretty well. I ate my meals at the training table, hung around and waited for an opening. Eventually, I asked if I could help out with spring football, and that's when I started coaching.

Times were very different in 1962. The out-of-wedlock birthrate was 5 percent back then. When we went recruiting and found a young person who was from a single-parent family, it was usually because one parent or the other was deceased. By the time I was done coaching in 1997, the out-of-wedlock birthrate had risen to 33 percent (it is at 39 percent today). In 1962, I had never heard of methamphetamine or cocaine. I guess I had heard of heroin (that was something that people in the Far East did) and of marijuana, but I had never met anybody who had used it. There was very little gang activity; actually, in this part of the country, there was none.

In the ensuing decades, things have changed dramatically. We see a great number of fatherless young people who come into the sports program, a lot more kids from single-parent and even no-parent environments. The drug culture has expanded and, of course, gang membership and violence has risen exponentially, even in the American heartland.

Writing in the early 1800s, Alexis de Toquerville, a Frenchman, said, "America is great because America is good. If America ceases to be good, America will cease to be great." America is still good in many ways, but few can argue that our culture has not drifted badly in many other ways. Our "greatness" is certainly being challenged. For better or worse, college sports have changed, right along with our culture—and I think we must take an unflinching look at these changes to honestly evaluate where we go from here. I believe in college athletics, and want to use whatever influence I have to ensure a positive future. Doing so is one of the most important aspects of my latest role.

The Players

Athletes are more gifted than ever, in several ways. Because of the increased academic requirements of NCAA sports, we see players who are more prepared now to achieve academically than in times past.

Specialization begins much earlier, too. Kids interested in athletics used to play multiple sports, but now, by the time they are in fifth or sixth grade, many have been pushed to choose just one. Parents send their kids to specialized sports camps. They give them the best equipment. They hire personal trainers and begin weight and strength training by the time their children are 12 or 13 years old. With this kind of early investment, it's no surprise that today's athletes are very gifted.

In 1967 and '68, Nebraska football had a couple of seasons that weren't very good. Our record was 6-4 both seasons. Some of us felt that something more was needed—we weren't yet sure exactly what—but Bob Devaney was amenable to change. About that time, Boyd Epley, who had been a pole-vaulter on the Nebraska track team, came to me with the idea of strength training for the football players. Boyd had gotten into bodybuilding a few years before, and had gotten so big and so strong that he kept breaking his poles. The track coach told him he ought to find something else to do.

At first, Bob and the other coaches and I weren't sure weight lifting was a good idea. The school of thought in the '50s and early '60s had been that weight training was bad for you. It made an athlete muscle-bound. We heard horror stories about guys who couldn't comb their own hair because they were "muscle-bound" (we'd never *seen* such a thing—but we sure had heard the stories!). But Boyd made his case, and Bob decided to give him a chance.

As far as I know, Boyd Epley was one of the first (if not *the* first) strength-training coaches in the NCAA. His program became a kind of Mecca for strength coaches. Over the years, he had more than 50 assistants who later went to other Division 1 schools and to the pro leagues as strength coaches. And it sure has made a difference. At one time, a 240-pound college lineman was a big guy; now you see kids coming out of high school at 270 or 300, with barely an ounce of body fat.

Players are generally better prepared academically and in better physical condition than ever. But they are also more troubled—not all of them, but an awfully large number carry heavy emotional baggage. Many of them live under enormous pressure to succeed, from an early age. Thirty years ago, very few parents planned for their children to "go pro." Now, you have parents who are extremely critical of their child's junior-high or high-school coaches, because they want to make sure their child gets the playing time they need to eventually get a college scholarship and play pro ball. Not only that, but these same parents tend to be very hard on their sons and daughters, pushing them from a young age to succeed on the field and in the gym. That kind of pressure can build and cause severe problems as young people grow into adulthood.

Fatherlessness also creates problems for young people, both male and female. The lack of a father leaves a hole in the psyche that must be filled with something, whether that something is athletics, drugs, alcohol, promiscuity or academic achievement. I've dealt with a lot of fatherless kids, and the vast majority have had a lot of hurt to overcome.

One young man, whose father had never been a part of his life, had a very strong sophomore season. His dad called me on the phone and said that he'd like to reconnect with his son, and would I have him give his father a call? I was pleased and a little excited—I thought that reconnecting a son with his dad would be great. So I talked to the young athlete and said, "Your dad called and here's his phone number. He asked you to call him."

The young man answered, "No, I'm not interested. The only reason that he's calling is . . ." and he named a few preseason all-American teams on which he'd been listed. "And now, suddenly, he's interested in being a part of my life. But he bailed out on me when I was a baby, and I don't want to talk to him." I was surprised. The hurt in this young athlete was so painful to see. Sadly, those feelings of abandonment and resentment are becoming more and more common among other fatherless young men and women—of which there are approximately 25 million in the United States today.

Performance

When I signed for the San Francisco 49ers in 1959, my contract was for $6,500 for one year. Today, I think the minimum NFL contract is more than $250,000, and the average salary is much higher than that.

I suppose that $6,500 then would be worth $50,000 or so today—it sure seemed like a lot of money. It was enough, anyway, to keep me from thinking twice about injury; I would not hesitate to run down the field in the face of large and very determined defenders. I wasn't a very big guy. Kind of thin. But injury didn't concern me, because I knew they'd pay my salary. If I got $6,500 for breaking my arm or leg, that was okay. There wasn't much money in sports, but I loved football and was going to get a chance to play with the best.

In 1959, my first year, there were only 12 NFL teams, and there were only 36 players on a team. Today there are more than 30 teams and 53 players on each team, so the number of players has increased fourfold. I was selected in the eighteenth round of the draft. The odds of my ever making a team were just about zero, but I didn't realize it at the time. I made it down to the last cut, and the 49ers asked me to stay on their five-man "taxi squad." We practiced with the team and hoped we would be activated. I roomed with Jack Kemp (who later ran for vice president) on road trips. The next year, I was picked up by the Redskins and played two seasons in Washington.

I think that, back then, drugs were seen as a way to simply play better, rather than as a way to play better to make more money. That didn't make drugs any less dangerous, but I think the motivation was different. Our team doctor, on one of the pro teams I played for, had a bottle of Benzedrine and bottle of Dexedrine, which we know now as speed. Both these drugs rev up the heart and the metabolism. The doctor would go around the locker room and ask the players if they wanted some of his pills before the game. I remember seeing a player nearly die in the shower after a game. He had taken five or six of those pills. It was a hot night. And the drugs allowed him to push himself beyond what his body could handle. He collapsed after the game. Fortunately, he lived.

Later, when steroids came into play in the late 1970s, there was not an across-the-board consensus that they should be banned—they made athletes stronger and faster, and that's an appealing combination to both players and coaches. But our policy at Nebraska from day one was that all drugs were potentially dangerous and not worth the risk. Period. We felt that steroids could be extremely harmful, but we had no way to test for them. The technology just didn't exist. If we saw a player gain 20 pounds or get a lot stronger in a short period of time, we took him aside to talk, trying to find out if the weight gain or increased strength had occurred naturally. We kept our ears to the ground for rumors about players hanging out in off-campus gyms, and encouraged teammates to police each other and keep the team clean.

When we started testing for steroids at Nebraska in 1984, it was the first year the technology was viable and available to us. We tested using Olympic standards. We tested randomly. We tested unannounced. And we tested in the summer—most players thought they could escape being tested in the summer, but we didn't give them any breathing room. It was very important to us, the coaching staff, to communicate from the start that use of performance-enhancing drugs would not be tolerated. We had one or two positive tests for steroid use, but we were glad never to suspect or uncover widespread abuse. Because our strength program was ahead of the curve, and because our athletes worked very hard in the weight room, we were a very strong team. One coach, whose team we had beaten rather badly, suggested in the press that our players were using steroids. A short time later, that coach's school hired one of our assistant strength coaches. That assistant coach later told us that the strength disparity between our team and the accusatory coach's team was very real, not because of steroids, but because the other team had a very poor strength program and lacked a strong work ethic in the weight room.

Later, of course, the NCAA and the Big 12 Conference initiated testing for performance-enhancing substances. I'm gratified to say that, to my knowledge, Nebraska has never had a player declared ineligible by an NCAA or a Big 12 drug test. Our athletes know that they will not play their sport for a year if they are found to have used any performance-enhancing drug.

I believe that it was well into the 1990s before the NFL and other professional leagues began to get serious about testing for and deterring substance abuse. Major League Baseball, yet today, is somewhat suspect; only in the last year or two have we seen a concerted effort to crack down. I participated in a congressional hearing a few years ago in which professional baseball players such as José Canseco, Sammy Sosa, Mark McGwire and Rafael Palmeiro were quizzed about steroid use in Major League Baseball. Some were forthright in their answers; some were not. I spent about half an hour alone with Mark McGwire before the hearing began. He seemed like a nice person, but I could tell that he was not at all at ease about testifying before the committee. More recently, players like Alex Rodriguez and Manny Ramirez have been linked with performance-enhancing drugs, which has damaged baseball's image even further.

I'm sad to say that performance enhancement seems to have been too great a temptation for many players and coaches alike, and officials let it go on for far too long. Now it looks as if the integrity of professional sports will be suspect for some time to come. It is my hope that lost credibility can be won back as athletes and coaches place a premium on drug-free performance, at every level of play. On a happier note, there has been a good deal of testing for performance-enhancing substances among Texas high-school athletes, and there has been a surprisingly low rate of usage. I am hopeful that this reflects a national trend and is not just a Texas phenomenon.

Recruitment

In 1985, Southern Methodist University's football program was given the "sudden death penalty"; that is, the program was put on probation for major recruiting violations. They couldn't play football for two years. The NCAA investigation turned up evidence of a "slush fund" out of which players were paid to play at SMU. Apparently, this practice had been ongoing for a decade or more and even involved a former Texas governor.

I have written elsewhere about the counterproductive effect of such practices. It is possible to win quickly and win big by cheating; however, over the long haul, dishonesty will usually cause a program to implode. When coaches, athletic directors and school administrators lose sight of the purpose of college-level sports—to complement and supplement a player's education—the driving force behind our sports programs is undermined. I was glad to see that the penalty meted out to SMU seemed to get people's attention, and am glad that the stiffer penalties instituted by the NCAA seem to have deterred other universities from engaging in similar gross misconduct.

Still, even today we often see improper and unrealistic promises being made to young people: "You're so good, we're going to change our whole offense for you. You're so good, you'll start for us as a freshman." And on and on. The quality of a university and its sports program should speak for itself. When I was coaching, we avoided making misleading statements about a player's ability or promising him that he would receive a certain amount of playing time. I have been pleased that Bo Pelini and his staff have taken a similar approach.

Many teams who have highly rated recruiting classes don't perform as well on the field as their recruiting rankings would indicate. When players find out they have been misled and deceived, they often either leave or lose commitment. If a team has a highly ranked recruiting class, but two years later only half of those recruits are still in the program, the team really didn't have a good recruiting year. On the other hand, a recruiting class that might be considered average can turn out to be exceptional if the players feel they have been dealt with honestly, buy into the program, and stay with that program.

On a related note, I am not a fan of the rising tide of recruitment services. The whole process has become terribly distorted. These services rate potential players on a scale from two to five stars. If you recruit a five-star player into your program, you've done a better job than someone who recruited a two-star player, because—according to the services' rating system—you recruited the better player. But there's a certain phoniness to the entire enterprise: Many times, the recruiting services don't rate players very highly unless they are recruited by many other schools—or unless the players have a financial tie to the service.

One young man who played for us in the '90s told me that, coming out of high school, he didn't seem to be getting much notice. So his dad called one of the recruitment services and asked, "Why is my son never listed as an outstanding player?" The recruiting service asked, "Are you a subscriber to the service?" The father said no, and the guy answered, "Well, send us $100 and we'll check him out." After sending in the money, this young man was suddenly rated as a blue-chip player.

This story illustrates why I am concerned by the amount of attention given to recruitment-service ratings and recruiting in general. For some fans, following the ratings is all-consuming. They get on the Internet every day to see how this guy is doing, where that guy is going and who is rated highly this week. Yet the irony is that Nebraska often played against teams that recruited many *Parade* all-Americans and other highly rated players—and we performed quite well against them, even though we recruited fewer "blue-chip" players. The high ratings of would-be stars don't win football games. Recruiting services do compile academic information on recruits and also make film clips available, which is helpful, but I don't place much confidence in their football evaluations.

We relied heavily on our own film evaluation of players rather than on the ratings of others. One such player was Irving Fryar. Frank Solich, our backfield coach at the time, spotted Irving on a New Jersey high school film. Irving was not highly recruited by other schools and was relatively unknown, yet he became an All American and was the number one player chosen in the 1984 NFL draft. Mike Rozier, the 1983 Heisman Trophy winner, also received relatively little attention out of high school, but he sure could run the football.

Money

I think student athletes are less well off today financially than they were in the 1960s. Back then, the full scholarship was room, board, books, tuition and fees. It included $15 a month for laundry (that $15 in today's dollars would be worth about $80 a month, which is a significant amount for young people who depend on scholarships and grants to attend school). We were also allowed to provide travel jackets for the players for road trips. At one point in the early '60s, movie theaters in town gave the players free movie passes so they didn't have to pay to go to a show.

Of course, most of those perks have been stripped away—the money for laundry, the travel jackets, the extra benefits such as movie passes. At the same time, athletic program budgets have grown exponentially. In 1962, the entire athletic budget at Nebraska was something like $800,000. Today, it's around $75 million. The salary for the first year of my contract as head coach was $25,000. That was in 1973, and I'm sure Bob Devaney's was even less in 1962. These days, many schools have coaches making well over a million dollars a year—some of them as much as $3 or $4 million. And facilities for athletics have been greatly expanded. Considering all this, it seems unfair to me that the student-athlete has not benefited more.

The federal Pell Grant has increased over the years, and that is helpful for students with lower incomes. There is also a fund set up by the NCAA called the Student Athlete Special Assistance Fund that assists athletes with emergency funds such as travel expenses if they have a death in the family and need to go home for a funeral. But still, student athletes were generally better off 40 years ago than they are today. The NCAA basketball tournament brings in billions of dollars in revenue to the NCAA, and I think we should distribute some of that money in a way that benefits the student-athletes who make it a success.

I don't advocate making athletes university or state employees, but I do think that athletic scholarships should be increased from the cost of education—room, board, books, tuition and fees—to the cost of attendance. The cost of attendance, which would include some transportation, some clothing and some entertainment, would be $2,500 to $3,000 higher than the current scholarship. But that's what it actually costs to go to college. The NCAA basketball tournament funds could take care of this added expense. This is a hard sell, however, as most Division I athletic programs are not self-supporting and there is always the need for more money. Still, if we see how that money is spent, we can make a very strong case for doing more for the student-athlete.

Academics

There have been significant changes over the years in academic requirements for college athletes. Back in the '60s and '70s, we'd hear horror stories about somebody going to school for four years and remaining eligible to play, but then having only 40 hours of coursework to apply toward a degree after those four years. They had taken random courses with no declared major and stayed eligible by passing a certain number of hours. But the whole point of their college career—getting an education—was overlooked in favor of "playing."

In the early-'90s, the NCAA began to institute rules and regulations requiring that players earn a certain number of academic hours toward a degree in order to be eligible to play—no more counting football or band as eligibility hours. Soon after, they began to raise the requirements to qualify for a scholarship, based on SAT or ACT scores and high-school grades. As a result of these changes, there is a lot more academic rigor infused into the system. Graduation rates have generally improved, and that's good—given the fact that earning a degree is the goal of a college education.

When I came to the University of Nebraska, we had one lady who monitored the freshman study hall. Soon after my arrival, Bob Devaney asked me to oversee football academic issues. I was coaching, teaching and doing graduate work, so I only had time to try to salvage those athletes who were on the verge of flunking out. There was no time to assist players who were not in immediate jeopardy.

Within two or three years, I began to hear from a nun who said she could run our academic program more efficiently. She convinced me, we hired her, and our academic counseling soon took off. Her name was Ursula Walsh, and she was instrumental in laying the foundation for a program that today leads the nation in Academic All Americans and NCAA Top Eight award winners and graduates 93 percent of student-athletes who have exhausted their eligibility. We now have a large academic and compliance staff headed by Dennis LeBlanc, a former track athlete. The academic staff is light years ahead of the limited troubleshooting I performed 40-some years ago.

Gender Equality

We've seen minority graduation rates go up as well, including skyrocketing numbers of women graduates in the last 40 years. Concurrently, with the passing of Title IX, we've seen a major uptick in the involvement of women in collegiate sports. Yet while Title IX—a law that prohibits discrimination based on sex in any institution that receives federal money—has made a positive impact on the inclusiveness of college sports, many schools are still in the process of shaping their programs to benefit female athletes without shortchanging men.

After Title IX was passed, three major tests of compliance with the new law were issued. The first is proportionality, which states that if 60 percent of a school's student body is female and 40 percent is male, then roughly 60 percent of a program's financial resources should go to women's sports and 40 percent to men's teams. This requirement became a real problem for schools that play football, because football requires large squads and significant financial investment, and there is no corresponding women's sport. As a result, we've seen a number of men's sports, such as wrestling, swimming, gymnastics, track and even baseball, dropped altogether to rectify the gender imbalance caused by football. These losses have been, I believe, an unintended consequence of an initiative designed to foster greater equality, but the impact has been very real and disappointing for a number of male athletes who compete in those abolished sports.

The second test of compliance, if a program can't meet proportionality, is to add opportunities for the underrepresented sex, rather than cutting sports for the opposite sex. Nebraska, for instance, has added women's soccer, volleyball, bowling and a rifle team to our program. There are no corresponding men's teams in these sports. Adding rather than subtracting is a good compliance solution for programs with the necessary budgetary flexibility, but schools with fewer financial resources may not have this option.

And then there's the third test of compliance, which carries with it some interesting nuances. An institution can demonstrate its compliance with Title IX by showing that is has met the need for and interest in women's sports expressed by its students. In

2005, the Office of Civil Rights, which administrates Title IX for the Department of Education, issued a clarification of this "interest and ability" test of compliance. The clarification included a model survey for an institution to use to inventory student input about the opportunities offered by its athletics program. It seems to me, however, that even with these more recent clarifications, this third test of compliance is rather vague and open to interpretation. It will be interesting to see how the various pending court cases that are based on the "interest and ability" test play out over the next few years.

For many years, the interest and ability test of Title IX was largely ignored. When I entered the House of Representatives in 2001, Denny Hastert called me into his office. Denny was Speaker of the House and also a former wrestling coach. He had seen hundreds of men's wrestling programs disappear with the advent of Title IX and wondered if I would be willing to explore options to stop the bleeding in men's sports while still preserving the advances in women's sports. I contacted Debbie Yow, the athletics director at the University of Maryland, who shared some of the concerns that Denny and I had. Together we did what we could to promote a more balanced implementation of Title IX. I don't know if we had any great impact, but eventually the Office of Civil Rights and the Bush Administration began to put greater emphasis on the interest prong of Title IX. We are still not entirely clear on what constitutes Title IX compliance, but it does seem that interest inventories, if they indicate that most athletic interests of women are being met, can be used to demonstrate that the gender equity concerns of Title IX are addressed.

Title IX has opened the door to a surge in women's sports, and female athletes have responded to the increasing number of opportunities by doing many remarkable things—things that, 35 years ago, few people thought they could do. Yet we still see some fundamental differences between how women and men approach sports. Anecdotally, we've found that women, more often than men, tend to come out for teams based on scholarship opportunities; men, generally, just want to play, and will stick around as long as you let them—even without financial incentives. The number of men who can compete as "walk-ons" has been curtailed in many athletic departments because of Title IX, even though they cost very little money. Men will "walk-on" in large numbers, while women are more likely to participate if there are financial incentives. I do not know if these differences are inherent or socialized or a combination of the two, but I believe they are real. And talking frankly about them as we move into the future of college athletics is important.

Looking to the Future

In my latest role as athletic director at the University of Nebraska, I will do all I can to ensure that our student-athletes benefit from their experience. Things have changed since Bob Devaney came to Nebraska in 1962—mostly for the better, and occasionally for the worse. As we consider the problems, dilemmas and hurdles facing the world of sport, I suggest that we concentrate our energies and concerns on the players as well as the quality of play of our teams.

Yes, Cornhusker athletics, involving 23 sports, is exciting, as many thousands of fans know, and the legacy of excellence handed down by Bob Devaney should be honored—with wins, as often as possible! But I believe the program will be strongest when the players are strong—in body, mind and spirit. The most daunting challenges facing sports are the same challenges facing our entire culture: fatherlessness, drug and alcohol abuse, gang violence, family dysfunction. As we focus on improving the lives of the next generation, it will be a "win" for everyone.

GOING TO WASHINGTON

Our doubts are traitors and make us lose the good we oft might win, by fearing to attempt.

William Shakespeare

Coach Goes to Washington

Why run for office?

When I retired from coaching, I did not envision a life of ease. The possibility of a second career in public service had been something I had thought about over the years. It wasn't attractive for its own sake—I didn't look forward to fundraising or campaigning or the almost inevitable personal attacks that come with running for office. As I've said, I don't enjoy public scrutiny and media attention.

In spite of all that, I had always considered politics as important. If you're the chairman of a big bank or a multinational corporation, you might have incredible wealth and influence. But if you're elected to represent a group of Americans in the federal government, you have an opportunity to shape our country's future. Education, taxes, the military, our economy—these are some of the most pressing issues facing America in our time. And even though politics can be difficult, sometimes very negative and personal, we need people who will tackle these issues with our country's best interests at heart. Many well-qualified people won't run for office because of all the negatives, but someone has to do it.

I suppose that I was somewhat of an oddity among football coaches in that I didn't read the sports page of the newspaper during the season, but I did keep up with current events in the United States and abroad. I was concerned about the direction our country seemed to be taking and felt that holding political office was one way to make a difference. That's why I ran for office.

Running for Office

I'd been out of coaching for about a year, still weighing my options. I had come to the conclusion that I had enough energy and drive to make a major push toward *something*, but I wanted to be confident about the direction I chose.

Some people knew that I was considering running for office in 2000, and many tried to get me to run for the Senate, as Bob Kerrey had recently decided not to run again. I considered the Senate, but it would mean six years in Washington, and I didn't know how Nancy would hold up for six years or more away from our children and grandchildren. I didn't know how I would hold up, either—so I was more attracted to the House with its two-year terms. I planned to serve more than two years, but if it just wasn't working out, I could quit after one term.

About that time, Congressman Bill Barrett, who had represented Nebraska's Third District for five terms, decided to retire. The Third District geographically encompasses nearly 80 percent of the state and is much more rural than the other two districts. I had grown up there, as had my parents and grandparents, and I was concerned about the unique struggles facing that part of Nebraska. Many young people were moving to urban centers, away from the farms and small towns where they had grown up. This migration—perhaps a third of the population from 30 or 40 years ago—had made an impact not only on the financial situation of those communities, it also had made the future uncertain for a particular way of life.

Even though I had roots in the Third District and attended college there, I had lived in Lincoln for 38 years, which was in the first district. Nancy and I did have a summer home in Ogallala, Nebraska, which is in the heart of the Third District, and we spent a fair amount of time out there each year. Still, some viewed me as a "carpetbagger" in view of the fact that I was not a full-time resident. Actually, unknown to most people, in order to be elected to the House of Representatives, you do not have to live in the district that you are representing. The Constitution states that it is necessary only to be a *citizen* of the state that you are representing in the House of Representatives. I have recruited, hunted and fished so often all across the state, particularly in the western part, that I considered myself to be as much a citizen of the Third District as any other part of the state. Fortunately, most voters agreed with me.

Although I had no background in politics or civil service, I thought that I might be able, as the Third District's representative, to help. Not everyone thought as I did. Some had pigeonholed me as a coach and could imagine me as nothing but a coach. But I was ready for my next role and was sure that my experiences outside of politics could contribute to my ability to be a good elected representative.

Consider our country's founding fathers. These were men who were farmers, merchants and doctors, not professional politicians. When they were elected to office, they agreed to go to Washington (or Philadelphia, in the earliest days) for two, four, six or eight years. They left behind their professions to serve their country, but they planned in advance to return to their families and livelihoods. The civil service model then was much like military service is now.

In contrast, there are young people today who start their "political careers" while still in college. They work on a campaign or two while they're in school. After graduation, they go to work in a congressional office for a couple of years and then go to law school, planning their run for their state's senate the year after they pass the bar exam. After that, it's just a matter of working their way up the political food chain, and before you know it, they have spent their entire lives doing nothing but politics.

Many of these people are smart, effective and well-intentioned. But I believe there is a great need in Washington, D.C. for people who are not professional politicians, who have spent a good number of years outside the political realm—people who will set aside their "real" careers for a time of civil service and then return home when that service is complete. I think that if we began to treat elected office in this way, there would be much less of what some have called "Potomac fever"; that sense of power and importance that makes it difficult to leave Washington. We would also benefit from the real-world experiences that people of different backgrounds and careers could bring to bear on the most pressing issues of our day. It was with these ideas in mind that I launched my bid for congress.

Two Crucial Decisions

When I decided to run for office, I chose to do so without money from political action committees (PACs). I would accept campaign contributions from individuals, and those contributions would not exceed $300 per person. I made this decision because I could see that special interests sometimes influence the way lawmakers vote by donating money to candidates' campaigns. I believed that staying unfettered from special interests would keep everyone honest: No one could lay claim to my allegiance because of donations, and I would be free to make judgments on particular issues or policies based on my conscience and the best interests of my constituents.

When I told people that I would not take PAC money, some got nervous. After all, many of the groups we call "special interests" are really coalitions of individual citizens who are looking for a way to be more involved in the federal decisions that affect them at home. These citizens come together to make their voices heard, and when their group donates to a particular candidate, it's not always to buy influence but to support the values and policies the candidate already stands for. PACs do, however, expect to gain special access to those to whom they have contributed. So when I would not take their money, these groups got anxious. One group asked if I would meet with them and listen to them if I didn't take their money. I assured them that they did not have to pay me to get my attention. But neither would they get special access.

Taking PAC money is a catch-22 for many candidates: It costs a lot of money to run for public office, particularly if you are relatively unknown. Getting the word out about who you are and what you stand for is not cheap. The temptation, then, is to take whatever money is offered and worry later about paying the piper. It's too easy for candidates to sell their souls for what they believe is the greater good: getting elected.

I was fortunate to have the option to pick and choose what money I would take for my campaign. I had "name recognition"—people already knew who I was, so I could concentrate on communicating what I stood for rather than on introducing myself. Many candidates must spend huge sums of money just so their name will ring a bell with voters when they go to the polls. In addition, it is much less expensive to run a campaign in Nebraska's Third District than in more urban districts because media advertising costs less.

The other decision I made very early on was that I would not speak negatively about an opponent. I would never run an attack ad, would never disparage or speak with disrespect. I felt that there was a way to point out differences on issues and ideas without resorting to personal attacks or innuendo. I wanted to focus on my ideas for addressing the issues that I thought were the most important. I'm sure that this aversion to negativism relates back to my coaching experience. When I was coaching football, our policy was to never bad-mouth or disparage schools that we were recruiting against. Some schools didn't reciprocate, but we felt in the long run that selling Nebraska and being positive about opponents was not only the right thing to do but also the most effective. Campaigning for office is similar to recruiting, so the decision not to go negative was a natural carryover from athletics. Attack ads turn people off, but most political advisors will tell you that they work. I just didn't want to go that direction.

My first year in Washington, Nancy and I attended the Republican Retreat held at the Greenbriar resort in West Virginia. The first evening, part of the "entertainment" was the showing of a series of attack ads that had been highly effective in the preceding election cycle. The candidate being attacked was usually shown in black-and-white grainy video with an uncomplimentary expression on his or her face, along with previous quotes or newspaper headlines that would be especially damaging. People were laughing and applauding these ads and how effective they apparently had been. I remember turning to Nancy and asking her if this was the kind of business we wanted to be getting into. Neither of us were very impressed by the whole performance but, of course, we had not been brought up in political circles.

Representing My District

I was elected to represent one of the largest districts, land-wise, in the United States. Nebraska's Third District encompasses nearly 65,000 square miles and has a population just shy of 600,000. People are spread out. The Third District of Nebraska occupies nearly 80 percent of the landmass of the state and is one of the largest districts in the United States that is not a single state.

Other sparsely populated states (such as Montana, the Dakotas and Alaska) are very large districts as well, which means that the representatives for these districts travel. A lot. The same was true for me. I spent three or four days a week in Washington and then flew home to Nebraska to meet with people in my district. I visited every one of the Third District's 69 counties at least once a year—usually more—and the miles added up quickly: 200,000 or so each and every year. I knew that in order to suitably represent my constituents, I needed to be present in the district. Sure, I had grown up in the Third District, but I did not presume that my experiences had taught me everything I needed to know.

Take, for instance, agriculture. You can't grow up in Nebraska without knowing a little bit about farming. Actually, I had spent four years in St. Paul, Nebraska, living with my grandparents during World War II. My granddad worked as a meat cutter in the local meat market during the day, but he also had several cows he milked every morning before delivering milk and butter to customers on his route. He had some pigs and chickens, and I can remember my grandmother occasionally beheading a chicken and cleaning it. So I knew a little bit about agriculture, but I was not steeped in farm policy the way I needed to be.

I also had to learn, very quickly, about education, health care, military families, water policy and a host of other issues that impacted my district in real ways every day. To be honest, those early days of listening, learning and assimilating great amounts of information were stimulating. Gaining new knowledge has always been valuable and intellectually interesting for me, and I enjoyed the steep learning curve required.

I think some people thought I would be tremendously frustrated with the slow pace of change in Washington, but I went with realistic expectations. I knew that getting things done wouldn't be quick or easy, and sometimes would be impossible. Yet, in fact, I was pleasantly surprised by what we were able to accomplish. I think three factors expedited things for me. First, I was fortunate enough to be a Republican at a time when Republicans were in the majority. That made it easier to get important legislation passed. Second, I had good relationships with Speaker of the House Denny Hastert and John Boehner, who was then Chair of Committee on Education and the Workforce (he is now the House Minority Leader). Those friendships gave me an opportunity to gain a hearing for my ideas that I otherwise might not have had. Third, I was not your typical freshman. I came to Congress with a coaching background that gave me an ability to get to know a great many members of Congress rather quickly. I was seen as something of an oddity and there was a curiosity factor, but after a few months the novelty wears off and people want to see how well you perform.

Equality and Democracy

As a culture, we have not always appreciated the contributions of women as equal to those of men. This is particularly true in the world of sports, but it reaches, I think, into every sector of society.

My two daughters were involved in high school athletics. They did very well, and I've always appreciated that they had the opportunity to compete—you learn something in athletics that you can't learn anywhere else, and it's just as true for girls as it is for boys. My maternal grandmother was quite a good athlete, a golfer and a softball player, who still loved to talk about her years on the field when I was a boy and she was in her 60s. But in my mother's generation and then in mine, women were encouraged not to play sports. My wife, Nancy, has told me about girls' gym classes, which they called "body mechanics," in which they did gentle stretching but never anything rigorous or competitive. I think the mindset at the time was that women were too frail to compete—which is silly, as my grandmother could have told them.

Title IX, while it has been a mixed blessing in implementation, was an initiative for equality that was long overdue. I'm glad that women are being recognized, on the field and elsewhere, as strong and ready for the challenge, because their contributions to our culture are invaluable.

When I retired from coaching and went to Washington, I came from a nearly all-male environment to an office in which all but one staff member was female. The truth was that I had never worked much with women, and I had a lot to learn. I soon gained a great appreciation and respect for the female staffers in my office. They had superb organizational skills, excellent writing abilities and clarity of thought.

To be honest, until that experience, equality wasn't on my radar. It's not that I was sexist; I just hadn't had much opportunity or need to think much about it. I'm sure I still have a lot to learn, but now it is important to me—whether at the training table with Nebraska's female competitors, in the classroom with female students or in the administrative office with my female colleagues—to do what I can to help women succeed. We are all equal in God's sight, and I hope to treat both men and women as significant and irreplaceable—quite a statement for a football coach.

The Iraqi Women's Caucus

During my time in Congress, I tried to go to Iraq at least once a year. Of course I wanted to meet with our troops and see for myself how the conflict was progressing, but I also was concerned about Iraqi civilians and how we might help them build their new democracy.

After a couple of trips, I was in a meeting with then-Deputy Secretary of Defense Paul Wolfowitz, Congresswoman Jennifer Dunn and a few others. Paul was briefing a group of congressional representatives on national security and Middle East issues. As we talked, I expressed some of my concerns: "Obviously, there had been an awful lot of war in the Middle East and many young men have died. I wonder if it would be a good idea to focus some of our resources on the women, who surely have a big part to play in Iraq's future." Both Paul and Jennifer were enthusiastic about the idea, so we began to brainstorm.

That initial conversation evolved with others' input and ideas and eventually became the Iraqi Women's Caucus. With some funding from the State Department, we invited women who were interested in being a part of Iraq's political process to come to Washington and other places to learn about how democracy works. Previously, women had been shut out of Iraq's elections, but in their first constitution, the provisional Iraqi government mandated that at least a third of the parliament's seats would go to women. That meant that these ladies had some preparing to do.

Congressional representatives volunteered to meet periodically with groups of 10 to 12 Iraqi women to share what we knew about running for office, representing constituents, writing legislation and negotiating with other lawmakers. But we also listened, and were overwhelmed by some of the horrific stories we heard. Every one of them had lost someone in Saddam Hussein's regime of terror, and many of them shared haltingly of children tortured in front of their parents or women raped in front of their husbands. It was unimaginable. They were so grateful that they were now free of Saddam's regime.

One of the cultural differences we had to get used to was Sharia Law, which is the Islamic doctrine that governs many people's lives. Under Sharia, women are sometimes seen more as property than as people. They are not allowed to wear Western garb and must always keep their heads and faces covered. Most of them don't have the option to be active, politically or otherwise, outside the home.

In one of the first meetings of the Iraqi Women's Caucus in Washington, I was introduced to the group as one of the co-chairs of the meeting. I went around the room and began to shake hands with each woman. But one young lady jumped back and refused to shake my hand—she could not touch a man who was not her husband.

Sharia customs and practices were and still are very prevalent in Iraq. I remember meeting in the Green Zone in Baghdad with Ibrahim al-Jaafari, the prime minister. He had been educated in Britain and had, I think, been in the UK for the better part of 20 years. He could speak English just as well, if not better, than we could. But during our delegation's visit, PM al-Jaafari only spoke Arabic and waited for a translator to relay his words to us. He was very formal, very traditional and very Shi'ite. I discussed the Iraqi Women's Caucus with him and expressed our hope that he would include women in the political process going forward. I don't think I made much of an impression on him.

Whether Shi'ite, Sunni or Kurdish, many of the women who formed the Iraqi Women's Caucus were well educated. Some had gone to college or graduate school in the U.S., Europe or the Middle East. But not many had been given opportunities to use their gifts and intelligence in service to their communities. Now they had their chance.

We decided that it might be wise to have a meeting of the Iraqi Women's Caucus in the Middle East, so we chose a resort near the Dead Sea and several of us went to meet with them. As I recall, more than 300 women came to that conference from all over Iraq. Most of them had come by car, and many reported being shot at on the way from Iraq to Jordan. They took enormous personal risks to come, and it was likely that their presence at the conference increased the danger they would face when they returned home. (Later, in fact, several women whom I had gotten to know were assassinated during their campaigns for office.)

Altogether we made four trips to Iraq, one to Afghanistan and two or three to Kuwait. We often met with representatives from the Iraqi Women's Caucus. Sometimes we discussed the upcoming elections and campaigning and other political topics, but we branched out to other areas, too. We offered some financial support. We helped them set up a number of centers throughout Iraq where women could learn skills such as weaving, basic accounting and how to start a business. All of this was done to empower Iraq's women to take their places as partners in their country's future.

It all culminated, of course, in Iraq's first free elections. People stood in line for hours to vote, and dipped their thumbs in ink to show that they had participated in the election. There was massive turnout across the country, even under the threat of violence, and I couldn't help but admire the courage and sacrifice of those who had struggled to make it a reality.

In many parts of the world, the poor way women are treated stands in the way of economic, political, social and entrepreneurial success. I believe that one of the major reasons there is so much poverty and lack of progress in the Middle East is that the intelligence, energy and creativity that women bring to the table has been excluded. Involving women in the democratic process and in everyday life leads to a healthier and less violent society and a broader appreciation for the sanctity of human life. Women play a key role in strong democracies, and we ensure a brighter future when we offer them opportunities to excel.

The war in Iraq has been very controversial. Stockpiles of weapons of mass destruction were not found. We have lost many lives and have spent billions of dollars, yet as I talked to Iraqis and visited troops, I was convinced that the sacrifice may someday be seen as justified. A representative government in which people are valued and productive may serve as a beacon of what is possible to other countries in the region. Entrepreneurial activity has exploded, women have been given a voice and the dynamism associated with democracy has been unleashed. Other nations from that region may eventually follow suit. Just look at the boldness of those in neighboring Iran who protested the apparently fixed outcome of the 2009 presidential election there.

Getting Some Things Done

Shortly after I entered Congress, I was approached by Bart Gordon, a Democrat, to serve as an original co-sponsor of a sports agent bill that Bart had been interested in getting passed for some time.

This experience made me realize just how important it is to have a champion from the majority party on any bill for it to have a chance of passage. Bart realized that as a Democrat, he would not be able to have much success with his bill in a Republican-controlled Congress without help from the other side of the aisle. Because I had a history in athletics, Bart thought that I would be a good choice to help him with the bill. I did so, and we got it passed. It was an important bill because many states had no laws governing sports agents. About all you had to do to be a sports agent was to say that you were one. You might not even have a high school education and still pass as a qualified sports agent. Because I'd been concerned about unscrupulous sports agents for some time, this bill was a natural fit for me.

I was also able to serve as an original co-sponsor of a bill that was aimed to govern steroid precursors. The over-the-counter drug androstenedione gained a great deal of popularity after Mark McGwire hit 70 home runs and then admitted to using it. Androstenedione is not, by definition, a steroid, but once it is ingested into the body, it has the same effects and is very dangerous. Before the bill was passed, any young person could go into a drug store and purchase it over the counter at great risk to his or her health. Congressman Sweeney and I were able to introduce and pass legislation that got steroid precursors classified as controlled substances that require a doctor's prescription for use.

The Farm Bill

Early in my congressional career, I participated in the writing and passage of two major bills. The first was the reauthorization of the Farm Bill. Because I served on the Agriculture Committee, I was able to add an amendment that increased funding for agricultural research, and I also introduced and had added to the bill an amendment that allowed for the burning of Conservation Reserve Program (CRP) land. Allowing farmers to burn CRP land was important for wildlife, because when land is burned, weeds that produce seeds critical to game birds spring up rather quickly. Once CRP has been established for a long time, the weeds tend to be squeezed out and disappear, and then the game birds disappear as their food source diminishes.

In addition to serving on the Agriculture Committee, I also served on the Education and the Workforce Committee, the Resources Committee and, during my last two years in Congress, I was on the Transportation Committee.

No Child Left Behind

As a member of the Education Committee, the other major bill I participated in formulating during my first year in Congress was No Child Left Behind, a somewhat controversial bill aimed at reforming K-12 education in the United States. With the help of Chairman John Boehner, I was able to get two important amendments in the bill. One was the Rural Education Achievement Program, which provided grants for small rural schools, which actually make up almost 40 percent of our nation's schools. Because most rural schools do not have grant writers and lack large numbers of students that enable them to compete for grants or get large amounts from formula programs, these schools did not receive federal funds to the same degree that larger schools did. My amendment helped level the playing field for these districts. The second amendment I was able to add to No Child Left Behind was nearest and dearest to me in that it had to do with mentoring. The amendment was called Mentoring for Success and resulted in roughly $50 million of annual funding to create new mentoring programs across the nation. This amendment has provided funding for hundreds of thousands of mentoring matches over the last seven years.

It was very difficult to get the Mentoring for Success amendment added to No Child Left Behind, as the Republican administration was determined to streamline the number of education programs rather than adding a new one. I was able to convince the committee that one of the reasons that we were seeing no improvement in graduation rates and test scores was due to the increasing amount of dysfunction that young people were facing in their lives. So many children are fatherless—roughly 25 million. Nearly one half of all children live at least part of their developmental years without both biological parents. Many children live in unsafe neighborhoods that are drug- and gang-infested. It is difficult to come to school ready to learn something when your world is crumbling around you. Such children are badly in need of mentors to provide the stability, affirmation and guidance that can be offered by a caring adult in their lives.

Underage Drinking and Federal Youth Coordination Act

I was able to play an instrumental role as an original co-sponsor for an underage drinking bill that was passed in the last year that I was in Congress. And finally, I got the Federal Youth Coordination Bill passed not long before I left Washington. This bill required federal agencies to coordinate youth services provided by the federal government. According to a 2005 White House Report, there was a great deal of disorganization within the federal government for youth-serving programs, which often created unnecessary suffering on the part of disadvantaged youth. Through the course of working on the bill, I became acquainted with a young woman who as a teenager found herself homeless. Because no federal youth programs were coordinated, she had to spend her days going from agency to agency to receive help; there was no single application she could fill out. Children in foster care receive help from as many as four different federal agencies. Too often, children were falling through the cracks due to the federal government's inability to break out of department and agency silos.

The bill also required federal agencies to evaluate each youth program and provide measurable, quantifiable benchmarks to determine the effectiveness of the program. This information would be valuable to Congress, as they decided which programs to fund and which programs to eliminate. There were many billions of dollars devoted to the 150-odd youth serving programs in the federal government. These programs were spread over 12 different federal agencies. I considered this particular piece of legislation to be potentially the most important piece of legislation that I was able to offer. It would deliver services more efficiently to children, hold programs accountable for performance and would be more cost effective. (Even though this bill has the potential to save millions of dollars and serve many more children more efficiently, appropriators still haven't funded it. I hope that this is the year it finally receives funds.)

Third District Projects

There were several other projects that we worked on. One such project involved Whiteclay, a very small northwestern Nebraska town located near the South Dakota border just a mile or two south of the Pine Ridge Reservation. I was approached by several

Native American leaders regarding the fact that several million containers of beer were sold to Native Americans in the small community of Whiteclay each year. No alcohol was sold on the reservation, so some Native Americans would walk the mile or so from Pine Ridge, South Dakota, down to Whiteclay, Nebraska, to purchase liquor.

Sometimes in the winter, people froze to death as they attempted to get back to Pine Ridge while inebriated. Sometimes people died because of alcohol poisoning—the whole situation was, and is, very distressing. The Native American leaders asked me to secure funding that might allow them to hire two deputies from Pine Ridge to police Whiteclay. The Nebraska State Patrol would occasionally get to Whiteclay, but it was far off the beaten path and not many people live there, so there was no regular law enforcement presence in Whiteclay.

I was able to get $100,000 in funding to hire and train two Native American policemen; however, the Tribal Council refused the money because they didn't think it was enough. Nebraska Attorney General Jon Bruning and I flew to Pine Ridge, met with the Tribal Council, and informed them that if they turned down the $100,000, the federal government would undoubtedly decide no funding was needed at all, and they would have a difficult time securing federal funding for law enforcement in the future. At any rate, we did what we could and they eventually accepted the funding, but the situation in Whiteclay still is not a healthy one.

On another note, as irrigation usage was tightened in Southwest Nebraska due to a compact with the state of Kansas, and as irrigation usage was restricted on the Platte River due to a compact called the Cooperative Agreement between Colorado, Wyoming and Nebraska, my office was able to secure a Conservation

Reserve Enhancement Program to take 100,000 acres out of irrigation in Nebraska and pay the people who retired the acres $125 per acre annually. This would help Nebraska gain compliance with irrigation restrictions that were mandated by law and would enable farmers who had land adjacent to streams to still receive some funding while they idled their acres.

We tried to encourage people using the CREP program to create hunting opportunities for pheasants, as Nebraska was once a major destination for out-of-state pheasant hunters. As farming practices had expanded, the pheasant habitat had decreased, and most of those hunters were now going to South Dakota. This represented a major tourism blow for several areas of Nebraska, and we wanted to encourage cultivation of habitats that would bring back these hunters. I was also able to get dollars for the University of Nebraska to fund research for more efficient energy irrigation practices.

Finally, I will mention highway projects. Since I was on the Transportation Committee, we were able to get funding for the Meridian Bridge, which crosses the Missouri River south of Yankton, South Dakota, and is a vital link with Nebraska. We were able to help provide funding for the Kearney interchange. Kearney is a city of roughly 30,000 that had only one connecting link to the Interstate, whereas most communities of that size have at least two and sometimes three interconnecting interchanges. This lack had serious safety implications, as an accident or some other catastrophe could be very dangerous and disruptive with only one road connecting to the Interstate highway.

I was also able to get funding for several railroad overpasses crossing the Union Pacific railroad along Interstate 80. Union Pacific averages about one train every 20 minutes on this route, as it is the most heavily traveled railroad in the country. We had several deaths every year due to dangerous railroad crossings, and these overpasses were badly needed. I was also able to get some funding for the Heartland Expressway, a highway that will eventually connect Denver with Rapid City, South Dakota, and will be vital to transportation throughout western Nebraska.

Earmarks

Obviously, many of the above projects are what have become known as "earmarks." Earmarks have gotten a bad name, as the term is associated with corrupt practices in which politicians seek projects for personal gain without going through the normal legislative process. Many earmarks are slipped into legislation without rigorous oversight and often without the author's name attached to it.

I believe that earmarks do serve a legitimate purpose, however. There was no one in Washington who better knew the needs of the Third District of Nebraska than I, as I was in the Third District every weekend and heard continually from the people across the District about their concerns and needs. Because of earmarks, highway funds that might have been appropriated in wasteful and unnecessary ways were targeted toward projects that had a high return value for the District. I believe that if a congressman has adequate justification for an earmark request, presents it to the appropriate oversight committee, has the request incorporated in a bill that is then examined by congressional leaders, passed on the House floor and Senate and signed by the President, then we have money allocated more effectively than if federal dollars are spent by bureaucrats who have no firsthand knowledge of the specific needs of congressional districts.

In short, with the help of many people who were higher ranking than I was, I was able to get some things done. This was gratifying, as often people serve many years in Congress without being able to get a single piece of legislation passed. Whatever success I had in this area was not due to any exceptional skill on my part. I was lucky; lucky to serve as a member of the majority party for my six years, lucky to have friends in leadership positions, and lucky to have help from the other side of the aisle and also in the Senate. Additionally, I had an extremely efficient Washington congressional staff headed by Erin Duncan, my legislative director, and Christina Mendeking, who administered the office.

Long Hours

Besides legislative initiatives, much of my job was to help constituents who had gotten caught in bureaucratic red tape. There were people who had been denied green cards because of administrative mistakes. There were military families who needed assistance with accessing benefits. There were senior citizens with questions about Social Security or Medicare. There were citizens who wanted to express their opinions about certain pieces of legislation, and there were always families who were touring Washington and wanted to visit their congressman.

I took this part of my job seriously—I had been elected to represent these folks to our government, and that meant being available to hear and understand their concerns. My days started at 8:00 A.M. and usually finished with a workout in the House gym around 9:00 P.M. I met with one group after another in 30-minute intervals, with an occasional trip to the House floor thrown in. On certain occasions when we were voting on a controversial issue, we would finish voting as late as 3:00 or 4:00 in the morning.

Empowering My Staff

When I first arrived in Washington, we drew numbers to determine which vacant office we could choose. My number was 39 out of 39 (there were technically 41 freshman, but the other two had special arrangements for their offices), so theoretically it was the worst office in the House of Representatives. We were located on the fifth floor of the Cannon Building, which could not be reached by all the elevators. Actually, the Cannon Building wasn't all that bad; John Kennedy once had an office there. The main negative about my particular office suite, Cannon 507, was that it was about one-half mile from the House floor. I walked three to four miles a day just voting.

I didn't do my job alone, and it was important to me that my staff felt empowered to carry out their roles. We had seven or eight staff members in Nebraska and about the same number on Capitol Hill, and in the early days it seemed they were reluctant to act on their own. Every letter ready to be sent, every meeting that needed someone to attend—no one felt they could go ahead and do what needed to be done without clearing it through the chief of staff or me.

It was obvious that, in order to serve 600,000 constituents, we could not have that kind of bottleneck. So I set out a general guideline: serve the people. If serving the people means going to a meeting or writing a letter or giving a speech, don't call me or the chief of staff to get approval. Do it. Go. You were hired because you're capable and because we trust you to make judgments about how things need to get done. If someone made a mistake, I would take the heat, not that person.

Every letter was proofread before it went out to make sure there were no glaring mistakes, but I managed my congressional staff just as I have managed other people over the years: Make the mission clear and trust people to accomplish it. I was fortunate to have an excellent staff of 16 people. Each person had specific areas of responsibility, and as time went on, we began to function effectively as a team.

9/11

There is quite a bit of disenchantment about "partisanship" in Washington. People ask, "Why can't Republicans and Democrats get along? Why is there so much bickering? Why can't they work together for the good of the whole country?" They can tell that much of the posturing and disagreeableness in evidence among Washington politicians is not for the sake of the country but in order to advance themselves or their party.

The sad truth is that the system is, for the most part, winner-takes-all. Whichever party is in the majority sets the legislative agenda and has all the committee chairs and a majority of members on each committee. All the minority party can do is act as "the opposition," doing its best to limit or modify the majority's initiatives in order to look better than those in power. The result is a highly partisan environment that seems to get worse as time goes on.

Having said that, I have seen firsthand how people with opposing ideologies can set aside their differences in times of crisis. The morning of 9/11, I was in my office in the Cannon Office Building when someone drew my attention to the TV, which showed images of the World Trade Center on fire. There was talk of a small plane that had perhaps flown off course and crashed into the building, but just then, the second plane flew straight for the other tower, and it became clear that what we were seeing was an attack, not an accident.

The alarm sounded and we were evacuated from the building. My staff and I walked 20 minutes to my D.C. apartment because we wanted to stay together and we wanted to make sure our congressional leaders could reach us. As we walked, we could see smoke rising from the Pentagon while sirens screamed. The Pentagon had been hit and many lives had been lost. Al-Qaeda had attacked not only the symbol of our economic might but also that of our military power. We only found out later about Flight 93, which had crashed in Shanksville, Pennsylvania, but had apparently been meant for the Capitol building, which symbolizes our government.

Nancy was in Washington at the time. Airports were closed, and people felt trapped. Nancy even looked into renting a car to drive to Nebraska, but I talked her out of it. Many people did leave by any available means of transportation.

That evening, we were all called to an emergency meeting. Speaker of the House Denny Hastert told us then that there were still 11 or 12 planes unaccounted for—those planes might or might not carry more terrorists intending to destroy themselves and everyone on board. We would be kept apprised of the situation, but now our country needed us to do our jobs with courage and determination. When the brief meeting concluded, members of both parties stood on the Capitol steps and together sang "God Bless America." It might seem melodramatic now, but at the time it was quite moving, and many of us had tears in our eyes. There was a strong sense of unity and devotion to the country.

The Power of Adversity

For three or four months after the 9/11 attacks, there was tremendous cooperation in Washington between the parties. Both houses of Congress seemed to be permeated by an atmosphere of solidarity—a recognition that, in the end, we were all on the same team. As unpopular as the Patriot Act has become among some people in recent years, we realized that U.S. law enforcement agencies must be given better tools to prevent further attacks. Whether or not every facet of that legislation should be kept on the books as-is, both parties came together very quickly to do what was necessary during a time of national threat and enormous pressure.

Likewise, we were all determined to do whatever we could to facilitate greater cooperation among the various law enforcement and intelligence agencies. One of the problems that became obvious quite early in our investigations was a lack of communication between the FBI, the CIA, U.S. immigration, the Justice Department and other bureaus, whether due to technology issues or turf battles. As the facts emerged, it was clear that, had there been collaboration between these agencies, the attacks of 9/11 might have been prevented while still in the planning stages—but because each agency had only fragments of information that it did not share with the others, no one could put together the pieces in time to prevent the tragic loss of 3,000 lives. Members of both parties saw the need for more cooperation between these vital agencies, and we passed legislation that included the creation of the Department of Homeland Security to make it happen.

When I was a coach, I saw that adversity often brings a team together. That's exactly what happened in Washington in the days and months following 9/11. We were all concerned about the safety of our country, and this patriotic concern was much greater than ideological differences or personal animosities.

When we debated on the House floor the legislation I just mentioned, I saw no evidence of one-upmanship or attempts to humiliate the other party; instead, people offered their honest opinions about how best these laws might work. There were differences of opinion, as anyone would expect, but these differences were aired with a genuine desire to reach a compromise rather than with veiled attempts to discredit the opposition.

Those four or five months were some of the most difficult and most rewarding of my life. I saw the good that a government by the people and of the people, when it focuses on being for the people, can do. Unfortunately, that time of cooperation did not last. The cloud of immediate threat dissipated over time.

We had the anthrax scare, and that extended our sense of common purpose for a while: All mail sent to senators and representatives had to be irradiated in case of anthrax, and that set us back in a time of great urgency. We asked constituents to email or fax rather than sending anything through the post because we would not receive our mail for up to three weeks, and the entire House of Representatives staff had to be relocated to alternate office space for a few weeks while the House office buildings were inspected after anthrax was found in the Longworth Building. But that crisis only prolonged a peace that could not be sustained. I suppose it was inevitable that, at some point, people would begin to think again of reelection—and campaigns mean "business as usual" when it comes to partisan politics.

Praying Together

Even in the rough-and-tumble atmosphere of party loyalties and personal ambition, there was one oasis of true bipartisanship in Washington: the weekly congressional prayer breakfast. I looked forward each week to sharing a meal and a time of prayer with my colleagues, both Republican and Democrat—it was one of the most uplifting hours in my schedule.

The speaker for each week's breakfast was a member of Congress. During my time there, we only made one exception: When Jordan's King Abdullah made a state visit, he specifically requested permission to address the congressional prayer breakfast. We were in a bit of a quandary because we had never made an exception before . . . but how do you say no to a king? In the end, we invited him to speak—and I'm glad we did. King Abdullah talked about the common heritage of Judaism, Christianity and Islam: All were born in the same area of the world and all consider Abraham, Isaac and Jacob their "founding fathers." Because of these common roots, he said, there are common values and ideas shared among all three; if we are to work for peace, we must focus on these commonalities rather than on our differences.

On all other days, however, the speaker was a congressman or congresswoman—and these folks were often very different from me, whether in terms of background, ideology or political positions. I admit that occasionally, when a colleague quite different from me got up to speak, I'd think, *I'm not so sure I want to hear what this person has to say.* But almost invariably, by the time he or she was finished speaking I had gained a new appreciation for that person, as the general format was to share one's personal life story—often with a spiritual emphasis, but not always. People who run for Congress are somewhat unique. Anyone who is willing to open his or her life to that level of scrutiny and is willing to be subjected to the criticism and the exhausting schedule of a campaign is not ordinary. You may not like them or agree with them, but they are risk-takers and are interesting people.

One morning, Patrick Kennedy, a Democrat who represents the first district of Rhode Island, was the speaker. Patrick was raised in Massachusetts and is the son of Senator Ted Kennedy. Now, I don't have to tell you that Nebraska is a long way from Massachusetts—not just in miles but also in philosophy and outlook. And my rural, middle-class background is quite different than Patrick Kennedy's upbringing. When Patrick got up to speak, I had a few preconceived notions about him. But as he talked with great honesty, warmth and openness about where he came from and the things he had experienced in his life, I began to realize that those preconceptions were nowhere near the mark.

Yes, Patrick was raised in a world of privilege and opportunity, but his life has not been a bed of roses. His "fairy tale" family has been stricken again and again by untimely death and destructive substance abuse—and every Kennedy misfortune is trumpeted across the pages of the tabloids. He has had trouble with substance abuse, and much of his passion to care for Americans with mental illness springs from his own struggle with bipolar disorder.[2] As I listened to Patrick speak about what makes him tick, I empathized with this young man and all he had dealt with, and I respected how he was making every effort to channel what he had learned from his experiences into something good. As a result of that morning, the two of us got further acquainted and, I think, developed a healthy mutual respect. In fact, we ended up working together on a piece of legislation that worked to provide suicide prevention screening for young people across the country, the Garrett Lee Smith Act.

The opportunity for us, regardless of party, to set aside our agendas and come together for an hour every week to listen to one another and pray meant a lot to me. It was a weekly reminder that Someone transcends our differences—and sometimes we could, too.

It's interesting: not everyone in Congress is a Christian . . . not by a long shot. But I saw the same willingness to pray together there as I saw when people gathered from all over the world for the annual National Prayer Breakfast in February. (I was an honorary host in 2006.) Every year, people from many different religious and cultural backgrounds come together in Washington specifically to pray. You might think that such a thing would be divisive, but just the opposite is true: When most people are given an opportunity to pray or to be prayed for, they'll take it.

The night before the National Prayer Breakfast, a series of dinners are held for people from many faiths from all over the world. As I talked with many of these people, they expressed an interest in Jesus, even though they might not have called themselves Christians. I found that there was an international attraction to Jesus and what He taught. To me, this was both surprising and interesting.

The Gym

The other oasis from partisanship that I found in Washington was at the House gym. The gym was well equipped and the door leading to it was unmarked, so many people didn't even know where it was. In the gym, seniority and party were set aside, and there were basketball games, running on the treadmill, using the elliptical trainers and lifting weights that occupied everyone's time and attention. I made many friends on both sides of the aisle during my evening trips to the gym. Many of us had no desire to partake in Washington nightlife (except those events that were required), so we would get to the gym sometime after 7:00 P.M. (and sometimes even later) and would often stay until it closed around 10:00 P.M. I've always enjoyed working out, and the friendships that I formed there made it an even better experience.

One of the people I met in the gym was Mark Udall. Mark comes from a political family and represents the Boulder, Colorado area. He is a Democrat and, politically speaking, quite different from me. However, we both enjoy outdoor activities. Mark is a mountain climber and has been on most of the world's highest mountains, including Mt. Everest. I am more of a fisherman. He has a great sense of humor, and as a result we spent quite a bit of time talking and kidding each other about the differences between Nebraska and Boulder, Colorado. Mark is now a senator, and I'm sure that he will do a fine job.

I remember Neil Abercrombie, a Democratic congressman from Hawaii's First District, approaching me in the gym and telling me that he wanted to celebrate his sixty-fifth birthday by bench pressing 300 pounds. Now 300 pounds is a substantial amount of weight for a 20-year-old, let alone someone who is 65, so I was a little concerned. However, as the day approached and Neil had trained intensively, I was in the weight room at the appointed time and was on hand to help if the weight proved to be too much for him. Neil strained mightily and got the 300 pounds up. I was quite impressed by the fact that this 65-year-old was able to do what he did. Again, Neil was someone who was not always attuned with my political views or I with his, but we got along very well and had a great relationship.

The two people who were closest to me in Washington were Jerry Moran, a congressman who represented the western part of Kansas, and John Thune, the congressman from South Dakota who is now a United States senator. All three of us worked out regularly and also saw each other at a place called C Street, where we often had lunch with other people who had a strong spiritual dimension. I found that John and Jerry helped keep me grounded in a place where it was often easy to get off track.

An Even Match

I was one of about a dozen people who met once a week with Speaker of the House Dennis Hastert. I think Denny related well with me because he had been an athlete and then a wrestling coach for many years, but I think he asked me to be a part of the group because I had a unique point of view: I was both a "freshman" congressman and someone who had been in an entirely different arena for a long period of time. I had a different life experience, and could see the happenings of Congress through fresh eyes.

When we met each week, we talked, as you might expect, about legislation coming down the pike, but we also shared our insights into the mood of Congress—how well or poorly people were working together, who seemed to feel marginalized or upset. And then we might offer our advice to the Speaker about how to handle particularly thorny situations.

On one occasion, I felt bold enough to ask, "Denny, why don't we let the Democrats win one once in awhile? Not every idea that originates with the Democrats is a threat to Republicans . . . and a few of them are pretty good! We should vote for legislation based on its merits, not on who initiated it." I was worried that many of my colleagues felt pressured by their party leadership to vote in a certain way to "get an edge" over the other party, rather than to enact good laws.

Denny responded by comparing the House of Representatives to an athletic contest in which the two teams are pretty evenly matched. Giving the other team a point could change the game, and the winning side (us) might never regain the advantage. I found this response surprising, because Denny was not, himself, a highly partisan person. He was very patient and a good listener, and I have great respect for him.

I'm sure that Denny's response was due at least in part to the fact that Tom Delay was the House Majority Leader at that time. Tom was a very powerful figure in that he was a prodigious fundraiser and had helped a great many Republicans get elected to office. Tom also was highly partisan, and proud of it. He was opposed to the Democrats having any kind of victory, and because he was counting the votes, he let it be known that he was disappointed in Republicans who broke ranks. Many people have painted Tom in a negative light, and certainly some of this was deserved, but I also knew that Tom cared very deeply about young people and had been very active in promoting many charitable causes benefitting disadvantaged youngsters. He had a hard side and a soft side, and at times I saw both.

I would hear 20- and 30-year veterans talking about how terribly Republicans were treated decades before by the Democrats. Some people had very long memories; they could recall, with startling detail, slights received 30 years ago at the hands of the other party. (I'm sure the Democrats had similarly long memories, but I only heard one side of the story!) All I could think, when I heard these recitations of past injuries, was that someone sometime must break the cycle of retribution and animosity. Nursing ancient grudges only stands in the way of working together.

Term Limits

This brings me to another thought, albeit one that maybe won't be too popular with some: I think term limits are a good idea. Congress is, as it stands, a seniority system. Ranking is based mostly on how long a person has been there—not on merit, accomplishment or expertise. And since committee assignments are doled out based on rank, the most influential assignments go to those who have been there the longest—most committee chairs have been in Congress for at least 15 or 20 years (and sometimes much longer). As a consequence, power is concentrated in the hands of a few people—people who have a vested interest in keeping it that way.

When I first ran for the House, I was asked to sign a term-limit pledge that would have limited me to three terms in office. I refused to sign the pledge, because I didn't know enough about Congress to have an informed opinion. As time went on, I became more convinced that such limits made sense. The longer some serve in the Congress, the more they become attached to the trappings of office and the power that goes with it. I also observed the effects of term limits on the Nebraska State Legislature. Some experienced state senators had to leave, but capable people always replaced them. It has worked well from my perspective, even though some very capable people have been forced out of office.

If we had some reasonable term limits, there would be a constant influx of new talent and new ideas. Yes, there would be a countervailing loss of institutional knowledge, but I think the trade-off would be worth it. We would have a government that is more representative of its people, and perhaps a greater number of smart and talented folks would give a few years of their lives to serve in the Senate or House, representing their home communities in the federal government.

Campaign Finance Reform

I also believe, as I touched on previously, that we need to reevaluate the part money plays in our politics. It's a very difficult issue to tackle. I voted in favor of the Bipartisan Campaign Finance Reform Act (also known as the McCain-Feingold Act), which was written to address some of the most troubling problems in our current system. The primary change was to the rules under which people or organizations could contribute "soft money" to political campaigns.

"Soft money" refers to funds that are raised to promote political causes or specific candidates without the person or group contributing the money being identified. As a result, a high percentage of negative attack ads that vilify candidates, often with untrue or slanted allegations, are never attributed to any one person or any one lobbying group. Therefore, no one knows for sure where these ads are coming from. Many people would not take seriously an ad attacking someone for opposing Second Amendment rights (the right to bear arms) if they knew that the money came from the National Rifle Association (NRA), which obviously has an agenda regarding bearing arms. With soft money, the viewer had no idea as to how much credibility to ascribe to the ad. McCain-Feingold essentially said that if you're an organization supporting a campaign, whether directly through donations or indirectly through advertising, you must be transparent about where your money is coming from.

My feeling was that Americans ought to take responsibility for their positions and not hide behind an anonymous organization.

If you have something bad to say about someone or his or her position, have enough courage to put your name on it. I voted for the bill. Not too long after, however, I was contacted by the NRA and the Nebraska Right to Life. Both organizations wanted me to know that they planned to downgrade me because of my vote on McCain-Feingold. It did not matter that my pro-life record had been 100 percent and that I was a hunter who had consistently supported hunting initiatives in Congress while serving as a member of the Sportsmen's Caucus.

When I asked how my vote on campaign finance reform had anything to do with Nebraska Right to Life or the NRA, they told me that the new legislation infringed on their First Amendment right to free speech. Well, all right, if you say so. But I think there's a problem when there are millions of anonymous dollars flowing to candidates from special interests. (The Supreme Court later ruled that most of the bill's provisions were constitutional and did not violate anyone's rights.[3]) McCain-Feingold had its faults and has since been circumvented in many ways, but at least it attempted to address a very real problem.

Ins and Outs, Ups and Downs

There are many more examples of special interests at work in Washington. We attempted to pass the Prescription Drug Reimportation Bill, which would have prevented pharmaceutical companies from charging more for a prescription drug in the U.S. than they charge in Canada or Europe. It was estimated that Americans would save 30 to 40 percent on prescriptions if the legislation were to pass. Essentially, U.S. citizens were paying for research, development and advertising for the rest of the world. The "drug lobby" spent millions of dollars to fight the bill by donating to the campaigns of several key representatives and senators. The bill passed, just barely, in the House but didn't make it out of the Senate. Time and again, I saw legislation that made sense for the American people undermined by the influence of special interests.

Occasionally, an industry lobby took a few steps toward negotiating in good faith. I worked on a bill with several of my colleagues to curb the marketing of alcohol to minors. Because I was so passionate about it, the alcoholic beverage industry was, at the early stages, nervous. A friend and colleague came by one afternoon and told me that he'd been paid a visit by lobbyists hired by the industry, and they had warned him to stay away from me, saying that I was a "bad influence." (I found this ironic.)

When we sat down to negotiate with them, I tried to make it clear that my passion for the health and wellbeing of young people had nothing to do with having it in for the alcohol industry. And I think they believed me, because they did seem to make some good faith efforts to compromise their position and to better enforce the resulting regulations against selling alcohol to minors.

On the other hand, we had to compromise too. For instance, there was in the original bill a provision to require research into the kinds of ads and slogans that would appeal to young kids, and to require that companies cease these kinds of campaigns. (There had been, not long before, an ad campaign that featured talking frogs, and many of us felt this was designed purposely to appeal to minors.) But the industry would have none of it, and that provision was pulled from the final bill.

Why was the alcohol lobby powerful enough to practically re-write our legislation, a common-sense bill that was good for American kids? Because they had contributed campaign money to a significant majority of the members of Congress! When I hear people say that PAC money doesn't make a difference in the long run—it's only $3,000 here or $5,000 there—I tell them that it's a debt that adds up quickly and comes due before you know it. And often it is repaid with interest at the cost of what is best for America.

Closing the "Nevada Loophole"

One final example: John McCain introduced legislation to close what is known as the "Nevada loophole," which allows gambling on amateur sports in that state. It is illegal in all other 49 states, which doesn't make a lick of sense—why should one state be exempt from the law? The Nevada gaming industry was raking in millions of dollars every year because of the loophole. During the NCAA Basketball Tournament, gamblers throng to Las Vegas to bet on college games. It is my understanding that the NCAA Basketball Tournament is the largest single sports betting event of the year, and there have been numerous gambling scandals involving college athletes. Unfortunately, it seems that it may take one or two more to gain the support needed to close the loophole.

John's bill had several major endorsers, such as Lou Holtz, Dean Smith, Bobby Bowden, John Wooden and a few other nationally respected NCAA coaches. Coaches realize that gambling on college sports can easily lead to bribing players to throw games. But the bill never made it out of committee. Why? Because the gambling industry had "invested" millions of dollars into the campaigns of a few key congressmen and senators. And it was easier to mire the bill in committee negotiations than to bring it to the floor for a vote, where those lawmakers would have had to justify their votes against the legislation. I don't believe many would have wanted to give Nevada a loophole that all other states didn't have if their vote were to be held up to public scrutiny.

People tend to be very good at rationalizing their behavior when money is on the line. I think they can even be pretty good at convincing themselves that they are doing the right thing, when they may actually be more concerned about financing their next campaign. It's too bad, really, because here is something that may surprise the average citizen: The party leadership, for the most part, trusts its members to vote their consciences. Sure, they want to "whip" the votes they need to pass legislation they want, but when push comes to shove, every representative usually votes for him- or herself and the constituency he or she represents.

Congress considers thousands of bills each year, many of which are very local in nature. In those cases, my goal was to support the local representative from that area, if there was no inherent Nebraska interest at stake. And, much of Congress' work involves so-called "suspension" bills, such as naming post offices, honoring championship teams, and the like. In those cases, I almost always supported the leadership. But there were times when I felt strongly for or against a piece of legislation, and I was never shy about saying so—and my decisions were always respected. (The leadership, however did *not* like surprises: If a representative told them he was going to vote a certain way and then didn't follow through when the roll was called, it was best if he had an escape route planned in advance.)

Freedom Over Comfort

It's interesting to me that the public often holds the President directly responsible for the economy. There are so many forces at work that it's difficult for me to believe that one person, no matter how powerful, is responsible for the health or dysfunction of an entire economy.

During my first year in Washington, which was 2001, we emphasized paying off the national debt. There were enormous budget surpluses and the accepted wisdom was that we could pay it off within a few years—the major discussion focused on how quickly to do so. Then the attacks of September 11 came. The World Trade Center was destroyed, the Pentagon was hit and Flight 93 crashed in Pennsylvania. Both psychologically and financially, our country sustained a huge blow. Congress established a new federal agency, the Department of Homeland Security, and added many other costly programs designed to protect our nation from further attack.

At roughly the same time, far-reaching corporate scandals, such as Enron, WorldCom, Global Crossing and Tyco, were uncovered and many people lost confidence in the stock market. This loss of confidence coincided with the collapse of the tech bubble, in which the price/earnings ratios of technology start-ups were sometimes in excess of 100/1. Investors had been buying tech stocks at massively inflated prices and were now left with next to nothing.

This trifecta of unfortunate events led to a very quick economic downturn. One might have been tempted to blame President George Bush, but the reality is that most of the contributing factors were outside of his control. All he could do was attempt to ameliorate some of the worst effects of the recession, and he did so by proposing tax cuts in 2002. I voted for those tax cuts. The economy appeared headed for a major meltdown, but we began a steady recovery before the situation got truly dire. I believe the tax cuts helped quicken the economic recovery.

We are currently faced with another economic crisis, one that is more severe than any we have seen in many years. Just as the President and Congress in 2001 and 2002 had roles to play in the restoration of economic confidence, so the President and Congress have roles to play today. But I think we need to be clear-eyed and realistic about what they can accomplish. The strength of our economy does not lie solely in their hands, and the difficulties they must deal with will not easily be rectified.

One of the greatest contributors to our economic difficulties has been unethical and illegal practices by decision makers in our business community. These people have been so focused on short-term financial gain at any cost that there has been a worldwide ripple effect that has been devastating.

Strange as it may sound, I think there may be some long-term benefit to the present economic downturn. We have become a very materialistic people, as a nation. Many people have relied on easy credit to purchase "things" they believed would make them happy. Some took out loans they could not possibly repay for homes they could not possibly afford. Unscrupulous lenders approved loans that should never have been made, and when thousands of borrowers inevitably defaulted, a crisis was triggered.

Our country is in debt to an alarming degree, individually and collectively, but such a crisis can lead to self-examination and a realization that God is in control, not us. We must ask ourselves the hard questions: Are we really as self-sufficient and infallible as we suppose? Is "every man for himself" a sustainable way of life? Will more money, more "things," lead to the peace and security that we want? Should we refocus our lives outward by serving others, rather than turning inward in self-absorption? Are we willing to give up our freedom in exchange for comfort?

An Inexact Science

How we answer these last questions has implications for how we want our government—our democracy—to work. My experience in Washington leads me to believe that Congress does best when it is focused on one or two major legislative initiatives, while it becomes fragmented and dysfunctional when too much is on its plate.

As of this writing, Congress has approved President Obama's economic stimulus package and his federal budget, which increases government spending by a huge amount. The President has clearly communicated his intention to propose major reforms to our health care and education systems and initiatives to curb climate change. And he is managing U.S. military operations in Iraq and Afghanistan. The Palestinian-Israeli conflict continues. Iran and North Korea pose nuclear threats. I worry about Congress's ability to respond with clear thinking and proper focus to the President's multiple, wide-ranging proposals.

With a huge budget increase and an exploding national debt, we are on a course for major government expansion. But does such expansion best serve the American public? I never thought I would see the day that the federal government would own and manage the auto industry, declare which banks were healthy and which were not, dictate some corporate salaries and move into areas normally reserved for the private sector. I saw firsthand how poorly government runs itself, so it is hard to imagine that government intrusion into corporate America will be an improvement. Regulation yes; ownership no. I'm concerned that our freedoms may shrink in proportion to government growth, and I think that now is the time to ask ourselves if that is a trade-off we are willing to make. Certainly, federal regulation and oversight of business interests must be improved, but too much intervention can stifle investment and entrepreneurial creativity. The increase in deficit spending alarms me. At some point, the piper must be paid; we can't just keep printing money without someday suffering the consequences. Many economists believe that high rates of inflation will be the inevitable result.

To me, it's common sense to say that ever-expanding prosperity flourishes in a free society. It is my hope that we will do all we can to strengthen our democracy and never trade it away for momentary comforts. President Obama and President Bush both took action to curb the economic meltdown. Let's hope that they got it right. Economic policy is often like coaching; hindsight is 20/20, but anticipating future events is an inexact science at best.

I pray daily that the President will be granted wisdom and sound judgment. He has a very complex and difficult job.

RUNNING FOR GOVERNOR

Politics has become so expensive that it takes a lot of money even to be defeated.

WILL ROGERS

A Tempting Offer

After I had been in Congress for almost four years, I got an interesting call from Karl Rove, who was then a top advisor to President George W. Bush. Karl asked me if I would be willing to be to Secretary of Agriculture. This call came totally out of the blue and was a great surprise to me. Karl said that he would like me to interview with one of the personnel staffers at the White House the next day. I told him that I was honored to be considered and went over to the interview. The interview went well, in that I don't believe they saw any negatives in my résumé. This led me to believe that I had a good chance of being appointed if that is what I wanted to do.

After completing the interview, I began to reflect on what being the Secretary of Agriculture might mean. I called Nancy, and we had a conversation about it. Nancy had been going to Washington less and less as time went on. Our grandchildren and children were all in Nebraska, and her friends were in Nebraska, so it was not appealing to her to spend most of the day sitting in our apartment in Washington waiting for me to come home late in the evening.

I realized that if I were offered the job and were to accept it, I would have to be in Washington for the remaining four years of George Bush's presidency. I would get to come home only once every month or two and would see my grandchildren very rarely. It seemed to be an unreasonable request to put on Nancy to move to Washington full time, so the next day I called the White House and told them that I appreciated the opportunity but didn't think it would be a good fit for me. This was hard to do, as a cabinet position is highly sought by many people.

That decision triggered a set of circumstances that was hard to anticipate at the time. Within the next few weeks, Mike Johanns, the governor of Nebraska, was appointed as Secretary of Agriculture and the lieutenant governor, Dave Heineman, was elevated to the governorship as the next person in line. This chain of events would eventually lead to my running against a sitting governor rather than running for an open governorship at the completion of Mike Johanns's term. As I neared the end of my third term in Congress, I began to realize that being apart from my family as much as I had been was probably not the best thing for me or for them. I also realized that as a member of Congress, you could get some things done, but most of the initiatives came from the Administration. Members of Congress were generally reacting to initiatives proposed by the administration. As a head football coach, I had been able to move the team in directions that seemed best, but as a member of Congress, I had a very limited ability to drive the ship.

I realized that being governor was more like being a head football coach in that it would allow me to initiate agenda items and make a real difference in a state. It would also mean that I would be able to be near my family more, so I considered running for governor, even though the lieutenant governor had ascended to the job. It was generally understood that this was what I was considering. Senator Chuck Hagel from Nebraska endorsed the governor and then later supported him with staff members, including sending his chief of staff to the state of Nebraska during the campaign, and also with fundraising in Washington.

I could sense that many Nebraska Republicans who had been long-time party members and who were known as insiders were not terribly favorable toward my candidacy. On the other hand, I reasoned that the sitting governor had not been elected but rather elevated due to Mike Johanns taking the Secretary of Agriculture position. And I did have some things that I wanted very much to try to accomplish as Nebraska's governor.

Performance Audits

I had studied performance audits that had been done in other states and saw that having outside experts take a look at the way state government ran often improved efficiency and generally reduced the state's budget by three to five percent. I thought that such performance audits would be very important in terms of controlling the cost of government in Nebraska, as Nebraska was a relatively high tax state, having higher taxes than almost all of the surrounding states. State spending needed to be curtailed and streamlined. Other states had reduced annual spending by 3 to 5 percent through such audits.

Warren Buffett, chairman of Berkshire Hathaway and one of the most respected businessmen in the world, had agreed to head up the team doing the performance audits and indicated that he would personally examine the way the state was investing its funds. Any organization would give a great deal to have Warren Buffett helping in the management of its finances, so I thought this was a great opportunity for the state. I also had a number of other business leaders and professionals who had expertise in areas such as insurance, accounting, education and health and human services who were willing to help with performance audits in their area of expertise. By reducing state spending, Nebraska could develop a tax structure more attractive to economic growth.

Methamphetamine and Underage Drinking Prevention

I also reasoned that underage drinking and methamphetamine abuse were costing huge amounts of money in the state; by my calculations, nearly $450,000 annually for underage drinking and in the neighborhood of $1.5 billion for methamphetamine abuse. Nebraska had a very large number of children in foster care in proportion to its population, and roughly one-half of those children were in foster care because one or both parents were addicted to methamphetamine. The average meth addict would cost society roughly $75,000 per year according to one study that I read, and a Creighton University study estimated that there were more than 20,000 people in Nebraska addicted to meth. Meth addicts commit as many as 50 or 60 crimes per year and are so debilitated that they are simply not interested in taking care of their families, nor are they able to do so.

While I was on the Education and Workforce Committee, we had interviewed task forces from various states who indicated that a concerted, well-organized meth and underage drinking prevention program could result in a 25 to 30 percent reduction in underage drinking and methamphetamine use. This could save the state of Nebraska $500 million per year in state and local expenses. It would also improve the quality of life for a great many citizens. The savings could reduce taxes or be spent on education, health care and infrastructure.

My congressional staff and I had spoken in nearly every high school and middle school in the Third District, giving PowerPoint presentations along with some fairly graphic photos of the devastation caused by methamphetamine and underage drinking. Nearly every place we went, we would have young people approach us after the presentation to tell us that they had experienced some of these devastating consequences in their immediate family.

We knew that these presentations made a difference, and we felt that on a statewide basis we could really ramp up the substance abuse prevention effort by increasing public awareness and making drug task forces more effective through funding and more personnel. The return would far outweigh the added cost.

Loss of Our Best and Brightest

A third agenda item was to attempt to stem the "brain-drain" from the state. Nebraska was seeing small gains in population, but most of the gains were from people who had not gone to college, and we were seeing a fairly large exodus of our best and brightest college graduates. We had initiated a number of entrepreneurial training programs throughout the Third District of Nebraska, reasoning that if young people from small towns were trained in how to think creatively, write a business plan, gain access to capital, write grants and discover ways to turn some of their ideas into reality, it would keep more of our young people in Nebraska. With these skills, they could develop businesses and be able to hire others as employees.

We helped many schools in our district establish entrepreneurial training classes. It was very encouraging to see many young people develop products and start their own small business. We also looked at ways to improve grant-writing skills and make people aware of grants that were available to start-up companies. Creating new job opportunities—particularly those related to technology—is the surest way to reverse the brain-drain.

Young people have always been a major interest of mine, and if one thinks about the future, it is critical to concentrate on young people, because they are the future. When the next generation fails to be productive, civilizations suffer and eventually die.

Disappointment

At any rate, these were some of the issues that I felt strongly about, and these were the circumstances that led me to run for governor in 2005. Many members of Congress who run for state office resign from Congress in order to have adequate time to campaign, but I felt that I should serve out the rest of my term as a congressman. If I resigned in early 2005, it would have meant either an expensive special election to replace me, or the Third District going unrepresented for several months. Weighing these possibilities, I decided to continue my work in Washington three or four days a week and then come home on weekends and Mondays to campaign.

This was a very difficult time. I was traveling a great number of miles and burning the candle at both ends. Football recruiting season had always been grueling, but this was even harder. I remember talking with Vince Dooley, the former football coach at Georgia, who had run for a Senate seat but abandoned his campaign. He told me that, for him, campaigning was like recruiting but seemed to go on forever. Recruiting was intense, but was over fairly quickly.

One prominent political figure called and urged me to run as an independent. Because Nebraska has a "closed" primary, only registered Republicans can vote for Republican candidates and only registered Democrats can vote for Democrats in the primary. This person reasoned that I would have fairly broad appeal for many Democrats and Independents and that this would offset some of the opposition within the Nebraska Republican Party in the general election. It would also mean that I would not have to win the Republican primary election. He may have been right. However, I was elected by the people in the Third District as a Republican and didn't feel right about changing parties for political expediency.

I lost the Republican primary for governor by four or five points. It was disappointing—it's always painful to work hard and then lose. In retrospect, I think there were three main reasons why I was not elected.

The Illegal Immigrant Debate

First, I had put my name on a federal bill that would allow children of illegal immigrants to receive in-state tuition rates at state universities. There was a similar bill in the Nebraska Legislature, and I was asked if I would sign such a bill. I said yes. I believe that it is wrong to punish or penalize children for what their parents do and most of these young people were brought to the United States as small children—they had no choice in the matter. And, in fact, if someone has the drive, initiative and intelligence to learn English and graduate from high school, and if he or she has lived in the state for at least three years and has applied for citizenship, that student should go to college and pay the in-state rate for tuition.

These were the requirements for the bill. At the time, there was quite a bit of backlash against illegal immigrants, and my position was portrayed as providing tuition breaks for illegal immigrants, not for *children* of illegal immigrants. Ironically, such children had always automatically been given in-state tuition rates as long as the student lived in Nebraska and had graduated from a Nebraska high school.

As of this writing, there are roughly 30 students in the university system who receive in-state tuition after coming into the country illegally as young children—not very many for the amount of heat this issue generated in the election. Because I have spent most of my life advocating for children, and because I was concerned about Nebraska losing college graduates, I couldn't take a position that would eliminate a college education for bright, motivated students who were in Nebraska through no fault of their own and who applied for citizenship. They would be assets to our state. Even though this position made sense to me, it didn't to many voters.

The Class I Schools Debate

Second, I had expressed some concerns about a few small, rural schools that cost many thousands of dollars more per student to run than larger neighboring schools. These were K-8 and were called Class I schools. This inequality didn't make much sense to me, especially because several of these small schools were within 10 miles of a larger school, where the average annual cost per student was much less and where there were more opportunities, such as sports and other extracurricular activities. But what seemed to me to be a common-sense position proved to be deeply unpopular in some of those rural communities.

As I recall, there were 28 of these Class I schools that cost between $15,000 and $90,000 per student, whereas the average cost per student in the state of Nebraska was $7,000 to $8,000 per student. There were eight Class I schools that had no students, yet most had administrators and teachers and cost taxpayers approximately $800,000 per year, with no one to teach. Some of these Class I schools received state aid, and many were very close to towns, close enough that students could drive (or be driven) a short distance and save a lot money. The bill, LB 126, was written in such a way that any Class I school that was more than 10 miles from the nearest community was exempt from consolidation and could exist autonomously because of the distance factor. This made sense to me, as rural children should not have to drive (or be driven by their parents) excessive distances to attend school.

As I traveled rural Nebraska, the number one complaint I heard was that property taxes were too high and reducing unnecessary school costs was a concrete way to address the issue of property taxes. On the other hand, many people in rural areas had attended Class I schools. Their parents and grandparents before them had gone to the same schools, so there was a strong emotional attachment and the issue became quite polarizing.

I was asked to sign a petition that would overturn LB 126, which had passed in the legislature and become law. I told those supporting the petition that I was not willing to do so. This proved to be very unpopular with many people in rural Nebraska. Ironically, the petition was not written well enough to achieve the intended result. The petition was intended to reopen those Class I schools that had been closed due to consolidation. But it was worded in such a way that not only did it not reopen those Class I schools that had been closed due to their proximity to towns, but it also closed down those schools that had been exempted from consolidation because of distance.

The petition passed, but had serious unintended consequences to those who were its advocates. The petition backers had almost the exact opposite result from what they intended. I'm glad I didn't sign it but my failure to do so was quite unpopular with some.

I found it somewhat ironic that I was portrayed as an enemy of small, rural schools even though I was very much in favor of those that were cost effective and served a purpose because they were located some distance from town. I had also done what I could for these small schools in getting the Rural Education Achievement Program (REAP), which was previously discussed, inserted in No Child Left Behind. Many of these small schools received thousands of dollars from the REAP money, which was so important to them.

I remember being invited to one of these Class I schools, a short distance north of Lincoln. The reason I was purportedly asked to visit was to receive thanks for REAP money that the school had received, which had been used to buy computers for the students. When I got there, I found a television crew and some reporters present. They were there at the request of those who were opposing LB 126. I was being used to gain publicity for their opposition campaign.

The media folks interviewed me about what I saw at the school and I agreed that the school appeared to be well run and that the computers were very important to the students. What I did not know at that time was that a great majority of the students in that school were transported by their families to the school from Lincoln. The children lived within proximity of many public schools in Lincoln and this school had become almost a small, specialized school that existed for a relatively small number of families. At any rate, politically speaking, my opposition to the petition did not serve me well in the governor's election.

The Learning Community Debate

Third, I opposed a bill introduced by a Nebraska state senator to split the Omaha public school district into three separate divisions. This bill was proposed in response to an initiative that would expand the Omaha Public School District by annexing 25 schools located in other districts.

I think the intention behind the bill to split OPS into three parts was to decentralize the district's power, but I and others saw what was hopefully an unintended consequence: The learning communities would potentially divide the district by ethnicity; one community would be primarily white, one African-American and one Hispanic. The NAACP, in fact, filed suit against state officials, charging that the law "intentionally furthers racial segregation."[4] The situation resulted in negative publicity for the state of Nebraska. But those whose local schools were threatened by the district's expansion did not look kindly on my opposition to a bill they believed would help them, and I lost their votes. Eventually, the bill had to be re-done.

Not for the Faint of Heart

When I first decided to run for governor, a politician friend said I should take a poll and use the results of that poll to formulate my platform. The idea was that I should find out what resonated with people and what didn't and then emphasize those points of view that had strong public approval while avoiding those issues that would result in losing votes. This approach did not square with my idea of leadership. It simply promotes the status quo; it has nothing to do with changing things for the better. I'm sure that had I conducted that poll, it would have told me to take different positions than I did on the three issues outlined above. However, had I done so, I would have been acting in ways contrary to what I thought was in the long-term best interests of the state.

So, I lost the election, but I did feel good about the fact that I tried to communicate what seemed best and gave people a choice. I also felt good about the fact that the campaign was run in a positive manner. There were no negative ads and I certainly did not disparage my opponent. I can tell you, though, that winning is more enjoyable than losing. In retrospect, I don't think that I ran a particularly effective campaign. I couldn't have worked any longer hours or covered more miles, but I could have done a better job of organizing the campaign than I did. So, in the end, I take responsibility for the loss and wish Governor Heineman the very best. He will most likely be re-elected and will be Nebraska's first governor to serve for 10 years.

I believe that politics is an important business, but it's not for the faint of heart. I'm glad to have moved on to a new role, but I still think often about the many smart, well-intentioned people who want, above all, to do the right thing for their states and for their country. Government is not perfect, and there are a few things we could do to make it run more smoothly and fairly. But I believe that many of the people who choose a life of public service are motivated by patriotism and a desire to do what's right. Those who are motivated by self-interest certainly tarnish the image of those who seek office for the right reasons.

Notes

1. Matt Daniels, J.D., PhD, "America Needs Involved Fathers," Alliance for Marriage. http://www.afmus.org/nav_fatherlessfamilies.html (accessed March 2009).
2. CNN Washington Bureau, "The Situation: Friday, May 5," CNN.com, http://www.cnn.com/2006/POLITICS/05/05/sr.fri/index.html; Stephen W. Smith, "Patrick Kennedy: I Wasn't Drinking," May 5, 2006, CBSNews.com, http://www.cbsnews.com/stories/2006/05/04/politics/main1590041_page2.shtml (accessed March 2009).
3. "McConnell v. Federal Election Commission" at Wikipedia.org. http://en.wikipedia.org/wiki/McConnell_v._FEC (accessed April 2009).
4. Sam Dillon, "Schools Plan in Nebraska Is Challenged," *New York Times*, May 17, 2006. http://www.nytimes.com/2006/05/17/us/17naacp.html?_r=1 (accessed April 2009).

Former assistant coaches Milt Tenopir, Ron Brown and I run (slowly) onto the field in 2007, before I was athletic director.

Johnny Rodgers, Barry Switzer, Chuck Fairbanks and me at the "Game of the Century" reunion at Oklahoma in 2008.

Shaking hands with offensive coordinator Shawn Watson.

Greeting Peyton Manning following my final game in January of 1998. Peyton and his dad, Archie, were gracious in coming into our locker room.

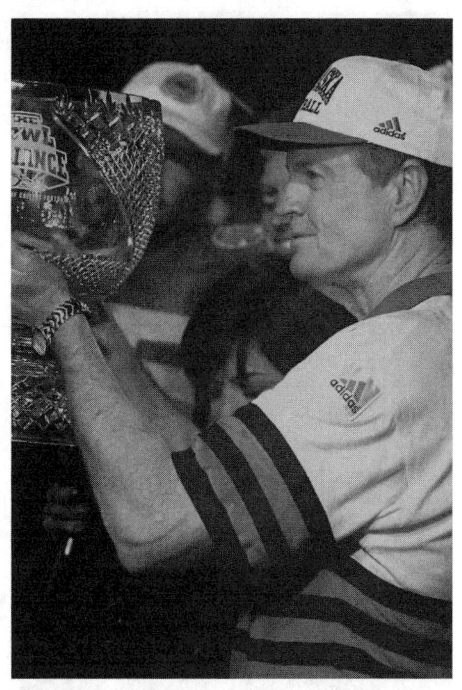

Holding the trophy after winning my last game as coach and the 1997 national championship with a 42-17 win over Tennessee in the FedEx Orange Bowl. (Photo © *Lincoln Journal Star.*)

Congratulating Husker Football player Ben Eisenhart on receiving the Cletus Fisher Native Son Award in 2007.

Presenting the game ball to members of the Lamba Chi Alpha fraternity, who ran the ball to Kansas State as a fundraiser for TeamMates. Husker football player Blake Lawrence and TeamMates coordinator Walter Powell are also pictured.

Congratulating Husker softball player Megan Mullin on her academic award at the annual Student-Athlete Academic Recognition banquet.

As athletic director, I had to make many tough decisions. So, it was a great relief and honor to finally hold a press conference to introduce Bo Pelini as Nebraska's new head football coach.

Me and my Washington staff

Nancy and me with President Bush and Laura at the White House Christmas party.

Nancy and me with my friend Denny Hastert, the Speaker of the House.

Speaking to an audience of women who want to learn about football at Football 101.

Me with Tony Dungy, former coach of the Indianapolis Colts.

Me with former mentee Cody Wolfe at his high school graduation.

Warren Buffett, Barry Switzer and me at a TeamMates event.

Nancy and I with Ken Risk, a TeamMates board member, on the field during an annual gameday promotion of the TeamMates mentoring program.

Me and Nancy.

My children and grandchildren at the Ak-Sar-Ben ball in October 2007. (Back row: grandson Will Osborne, son Mike Osborne, son-in-law Jason Hince, daughter Ann Wilke, son-in-law Bob Wilke. Front row: daughter-in-law Emily Osborne, granddaughter Catey Osborne, daughter Suzanne Hince, granddaughter Haley Wilke, grandson Christian Wilke.) (Photo © MDP Dwyer Photography.)

Me fishing in the Bow River in Banff National Park in Alberta, Canada.

Me with son, Mike, grandson Will and our friends Rich and Karen Teague in Alaska on a fishing trip.

RETURNING TO NEBRASKA

It's not over until it's over.

Yogi Berra

Coaching Coaches

Prior to my return to Nebraska as athletic director, a consultant from the business world was hired to evaluate the athletic department. I think the idea was to improve performance, but things didn't seem to be working out well. Even though the consultant had been in the athletic department only 10 weeks, he was seeking to make some major changes. He was from the business world and had no specific knowledge of athletic departments. He required administrators to report to him rather than to the athletic director, reviewed emails that were sent out to make sure they were to his liking, and also had many closed-door meetings. As a result, a certain amount of mistrust had begun to pervade the athletic department.

This consultant was in the process of setting up a fairly elaborate system of evaluation and performance reviews, which would have taken a great deal of time to implement. The reviews would occur every 90 days, and cost of living raises would then be allocated based on those reviews. The only problem was that this particular plan would have been contrary to University policy. The situation had become somewhat dysfunctional, in that people were fearful for their jobs and no one felt very free to operate on their own initiative without first checking with the consultant. In the day or so that intervened between the previous athletic director's dismissal and my being hired, the staff fired the consultant, which was a fairly good indicator of how unpopular some of his reforms had been.

Part of my job, in my latest role, is to coach the athletic department staff. I want to see good effort and standout performance, but I also want to create an enjoyable place to work. Putting good people under the gun to ratchet up their level of accomplishment from one day to the next is, in my experience, not the best way to get the best out of them. Instead of creating a team-oriented environment that encourages collaboration and mutual trust, excessive focus on individual performance fosters unhealthy competition, division and dysfunction.

The damage done to the staff has taken a number of months to repair—such a high level of stress had stretched some almost to the breaking point, and unwinding the tension couldn't happen overnight. But, I'm pleased to report, the coaches and staff at the University of Nebraska are resilient and focused. There is a growing sense of teamwork and support among departments and coaches, and people tell me they feel much better about going to work every day.

Back in the Arena

The opportunity to lead such a talented staff comes with its share of pros and cons.

When I was asked to return to Nebraska, my wife, Nancy, and I both struggled with the decision. Part of the struggle was due to the realization that I would be taking a position that would again entail a great deal of public scrutiny, including events to attend, press interviews and meetings with alumni and boosters. After 36 years of coaching and six years in the U.S. Congress, both Nancy and I were ready to retreat into the background, at least somewhat removed from view.

After leaving Congress, I spent a semester teaching leadership classes in the university's College of Business. I arranged my teaching schedule so that long weekends were possible, taking off Friday through Monday and teaching Tuesday through Thursday. Nancy and I enjoyed the opportunity to spend more time together, and I was glad to have time for fishing, hunting and grandchildren.

I have always enjoyed teaching. I taught several sections of educational psychology and a section of statistics when I was doing graduate work in the mid-1960s, and I enjoyed it so much that it made my decision to go into coaching more difficult. I always felt that coaching was primarily teaching. You were not only teaching *X*s and *O*s but also teaching principles by which young people could deal with adversity, success, fame and fortune later on in their lives.

I found the College of Business to be open to my coming there in 2007. At first, I was afraid that some of the faculty might resent my sudden appearance, but this didn't seem to be the case. I was very impressed by the quality of faculty and of the students. I was teaching seniors in the College of Business Administration, along with a few graduate students, and the primary topic was leadership. Most of these students had a pretty good idea of where they were headed and were intelligent and quite focused. I have always felt energized by interaction with young people, and I enjoyed those two semesters very much.

When I was asked to become the athletic director in the middle of the second semester of teaching , it presented a problem, as I was trying to get my feet on the ground in the athletic department and yet didn't feel right about leaving my approximately 80 students in the middle of the semester. I did have two or three occasions on which I had guest lecturers substitute for me; however, I was in class most of the time, and I graded papers and administered the final exam. The students appreciated the fact that I stayed with them. I enjoyed interacting with them; however, it was a packed schedule with me trying to become athletics director and working with a 2007 football season that was headed south.

When the call to serve as athletics director came, Nancy and I both knew what we'd be getting into, having been there before. But together we decided that, if we could be of help, we wanted to make a contribution because athletics is so important to the state of Nebraska.

I enjoy an evening at home; not having a social event on the calendar is always a welcome relief. I am, socially speaking, almost the exact opposite of Bob Devaney, who was one of the most outgoing personalities I've ever known. After every home game, you could find Bob and his wife, Phyllis, at the American Legion Club in Lincoln. Bob would have dinner, dance with his wife, and generally hold court with the fans until the wee hours of the morning.

When I was coaching, though, I wasn't much of a social butterfly (and I'm still not). After a week of preparation and a hard-fought game, I looked forward to heading home. I usually turned on the film projector between 10 and 11 PM, and graded our team's performance until about 2 AM. This allowed me to spend Sunday morning with my family and to attend church. By 1 PM on Sunday, we started our preparation for the next opponent and spent 80 to 90 hours getting ready for the next game.

When I was asked in October 2007 to become Nebraska's athletic director, I knew that, in the same month, I was also to be named King of Ak-Sar-Ben ("Nebraska" spelled backward). The Knights of Ak-Sar-Ben Foundation, although it reaches across the state, is particularly important to people in Omaha. A year as King of Ak-Sar-Ben meant attending a large number of social events as well as being featured at the Ak-Sar-Ben Coronation Ball—for which I dressed up in Renaissance-style finery, including tights!

Not being much of a showman, I admit that marching down the aisle at the ball was one of my more uncomfortable moments. Settling in as athletic director in the same year as my obligations to Ak-Sar-Ben proved to be a somewhat taxing experience for someone who was contemplating a less active lifestyle.

I am always honored when people want to take a picture with me or want my autograph. I must admit, however, that there are times—especially when I am having dinner with my family or am engaged in conversation—when such requests can be somewhat bothersome. I never refuse such requests, though, unless I am late for an appointment. Sometimes people put me on the spot by asking if I remember their name or if I remember when we were together on the elevator at the Cornhusker Hotel in 1985. Of course, I often don't remember, and it is difficult to answer in a way that won't offend.

Being a rather private person, I am not particularly good at small talk and have to work at it—I can hold my own at a reception or dinner, but it does not come naturally. During my early years as head coach, people often commented (not unkindly) about how different I am from Bob Devaney: He was always quite at home in the public eye, while I often appeared to be uncomfortable and looking for an exit.

All in all, having some measure of celebrity is both good and bad. I have never viewed myself as someone who deserves special attention, but I realize that some notoriety comes with having a position such as head football coach, congressman or athletics director. For me, the increased scrutiny and demands on my time are worth the opportunity to invest in the lives of student-athletes and their coaches.

It would just be easier if I was more fond of life in the public eye.

The Pink Slip

I never thought I'd have to fire a coach. Unfortunately, my latest role demands a willingness to make unpleasant decisions.

When Bill Callahan and his staff arrived in 2004, Turner Gill, the only holdover from Frank Solich's and my staff, asked me to talk to the new staff and explain those things pertaining to Nebraska football that were especially important and unique. I spent more than two hours reviewing the importance of walk-ons, how the Unity Council came to be and how it worked, the importance of goal setting, the philosophy behind our offense and defense, and our recruiting strategies and the uniqueness of our fan base. The staff listened politely, but I didn't think that much of anything I talked about gained much traction. I had the impression that previous NFL and college experience trumped anything that I had to offer.

I met with the football coaching staff again shortly after being named athletic director, and I told them that I would do anything I could do to support them. I was up front about the fact that we needed to win seven or eight games in the season at hand. If we could do that, then everything would be fine—we would rebuild the program from there. On the other hand, if the team only broke even or, worse, had another losing season, I would likely make some staffing changes. With that said, what could I do to help?

Some people have speculated that I was hired to fire Bill Callahan. This was not the case. I didn't know Bill well and had no animosity toward him. On the other hand, as I mentioned previously, I could sense that things weren't going well. I was sincere in wanting Bill and his staff to succeed. A coach hates to fire another coach.

We began to lose, and lose badly. As we went along, I met with the coaches every week or so to find out what they needed and to give input when I was asked. We lost the last game of the season to Colorado, which gave us a 5-7 record. The most disappointing thing about the season wasn't the seven losses, however, but the fact that as the season progressed, the players seemed to lose confidence and, at times, didn't play with intensity. This was distressing to those who cared about Nebraska football, as we had almost always been an excellent team as far as commitment and effort were concerned. Our team played hard in losing to Texas and played well in defeating Kansas State, but we weren't very competitive in our games with USC, Missouri, Oklahoma State, Texas A&M, Kansas and Colorado, so the die was cast.

I met with head coach Bill Callahan the Monday morning following the Colorado game and told him that, under the circumstances, I would not renew his contract. I thought we needed to make a change. Then I sat down with each of the assistant coaches and told them that I would do whatever I could to help them find new jobs. There was a chance that the new head coach would ask some of them to stay, but it was not for me to decide. (In fact, two of them were asked to stay on after I hired Bo Pelini.)

When people read the sports pages and see that a coach is leaving, they often don't realize that many other people also lose their jobs: assistant coaches, sometimes administrative assistants, strength coaches and others. When I resigned as head coach after the 1997 season, I made sure that the staff would remain for at least one year. This seldom happens in major college athletics, and I was fortunate to be in a position in which I could ensure the job security of those I was leaving behind. Likewise, when Bob Devaney stepped down in 1973, he made sure that everyone on his staff had a job. When I handed the job over to Frank Solich in 1998, there was a thread of continuity from 1962 until Frank's dismissal in 2003.

Next, I began a search for a new head football coach. After interviewing five coaches, the right choice became clear to me. Bo Pelini had been at Nebraska in 2003 as a defensive coordinator, and I had positive recommendations from both players and coaches who had worked with him then. From his time at Nebraska, at Oklahoma and then at Louisiana State, Bo had earned a reputation as a very good defensive coach—and that's where our team was most deficient.

I asked Chancellor Perlman if he would like to accompany me on a trip to Baton Rouge to interview Bo Pelini and then on to Atlanta, where a search firm would have four other head coaches for us to interview. We accomplished the interviews over a two-day period and talked to several men who had experienced considerable success as head coaches and had staffs of assistants already in place. Even though Bo Pelini wasn't a head coach, I chose him because I felt we needed to make a significant turnaround on defense. We had lost several games by large margins in the 2007 season, and we had a number of great offensive teams in the Big 12 that would be returning most of their starters and their quarterbacks in 2008. If we couldn't slow those people down, we would likely have another losing season, and then things would be in danger of unraveling badly.

Members of the media were quite interested in the hiring process, so they were tracking the tail number on the airplane we flew to Baton Rouge and Atlanta. It was reported that the plane had abruptly dropped several thousand feet—I don't remember this happening, but it did catch the attention of our families.

Most coaches don't want their names mentioned in connection with a job search, so the interviews in Atlanta were very private. Any information as to who was interviewed did not come from Nebraska or the search firm we employed.

It was difficult not to hire Turner Gill, who was head coach at the University of Buffalo. Turner had played for me and had coached for me for a number of years as an assistant. I was in his wedding. Turner had been at Buffalo for two years and had begun to turn that program around. However, I knew that Turner's main experience and expertise as a coach was on the offensive side of the ball, which was not an area where we needed the most help. I felt that Shawn Watson, the offensive coordinator under Bill Callahan, would be able to handle the offense well, so I had to look at who would do the best job of bringing the defense along and also be able to run the whole program effectively.

Telling Turner that I was not going to hire him was one of the hardest things I have had to do. I know that Turner wanted the job, understood the culture at Nebraska, and was someone who was a great person and a great role model. Turner staying at Buffalo, however, was great for that program, as he managed to win the Mid-American Conference this past year and go to a bowl game. This was the first championship and the first bowl game for Buffalo in a generation. Turner will do well and will have many opportunities ahead of him.

I never imagined myself in a position to fire coaches–I had always *been* a coach, and I know firsthand how difficult a job coaching is. Letting Coach Callahan go was painful, but I felt that doing so was in the best long-term interest of Nebraska's football program. I tried to manage the transition as smoothly as possible, to minimize hurt feelings and bruised egos through a time of uncertainty and upheaval. I hope those involved see it that way, too.

Bo Pelini was our new head coach. Now to get out of the way . . .

A Focus on Values

When I was head coach, I tried not to micromanage my assistants. If an offensive coach had drills that he preferred to run, great—attending to that kind of detail was his job, and he could do so with a certain level of autonomy. My job was to attend to the larger principles that would create a healthy environment and winning football team.

I approach my latest role in the same way. I try very hard not to micromanage. Instead, it's my goal to make space for coaches and others to use their own talents and energy to create solid, successful teams. I try to do this by setting guidelines based on core values, such as integrity, trust, respect, teamwork and loyalty.

For example, *respect* is a core value of our program. To foster an atmosphere of respect in which everyone—both players and coaches—can achieve his or her best, we have general guidelines for how student athletes and staff will be treated within the program. We don't humiliate people. We don't denigrate them. We don't tear people down. It's my job to help coaches lead effectively within these guidelines, not to tell them to do a particular drill or run a certain play.

I want to be available to our staff, to help them in whatever ways I can. I am honored to work with a talented and dynamic group of leaders, and feel privileged to mentor, even in a small way, the next great generation of coaches. The drills, plays and formations will change and evolve as time goes on, but focusing on values is always a winning strategy. That focus is what I want to pass on.

Leaving a Legacy

Let's face it: In Nebraska, we were spoiled. Over a 42-year time span, going back to 1962 and ending in 2003, the Cornhuskers had won 82 percent of our games—by far the highest percentage of any program in the country for that same period of time. We had no losing seasons during those 42 years, went to 40 bowl games, and won 25 conference championships and five national championships.

Bob Devaney, who turned the program around, coached for 11 years. I coached for 25 years. Frank Solich coached the last 6 years of that 42-year period. During Frank's tenure, his record was 9-4, 12-1, 10-2, 11-2, 7-7 and 9-3 (10-3 if you count the bowl win after he was fired). He won a Big 12 Championship, played for a national championship in the Rose Bowl, played in 2 BCS bowl games, and went to 6 straight bowls. This is an excellent record by any standard. The circumstance that made Frank's job so difficult was that we had gone 60-3 with 3 national championships in the 5 seasons prior to his taking over as coach. While others might have had a different perspective, in my view the expectations had become totally unrealistic. Frank's record was very much in line with Bob's first 8 years and my first 20 years. The odds of a confluence of talent and team chemistry occurring again as they did during my last 5 seasons were just about zero no matter who was coaching, yet that was the standard to which many held him.

Some fans came to believe that the best high school players in the nation would always come to Nebraska—because, after all, *it's Nebraska*—and that we would always win. They believed that there was something magical about Lincoln and football, and forgot about how fragile success in athletics is.

Then, all of the sudden, those same people realized that winning football games isn't automatic. Long-standing success is more precarious than they had ever imagined. And that realization was difficult for fans to deal with, just as it was difficult for UCLA basketball fans after head coach John Wooden retired in 1975 and the Bruins no longer won their way to the NCAA finals every year. It was difficult for me to watch Nebraska fans struggle through several very long winters, even though I knew that football, like other sports, is cyclical. My sadness was not a matter of "What happened to the program we had built?" Rather, it was painful for me to see Nebraska fans experience such disappointment. Two losing seasons out of four was a rude awakening.

It seems to me that some people are very conscious about leaving a legacy. You sometimes hear about a president's concern over how history will remember him, and about his efforts to get things done the last year or two he is in office in order to make his mark in a particular way. Or you hear about an actor who wants to be seen as creative or expressive or shocking, and chooses to work on a film based on how it might affect how he or she is remembered. For a politician, his or her legislative initiatives, peace accords and economic proposals all play a part in the quest for a legacy. I guess for authors, it's the number of books sold or the number of times on the bestseller lists. In the same way, coaches concerned with legacy often focus on their win-loss records.

I never thought too much about leaving a legacy as it related to wins and losses. I remember talking years ago to Ron Brown, one of our coaches at Nebraska and host of *Sharing the Victory*, the national radio show produced by the Fellowship of Christian Athletes. Ron told me, "Your legacy is not going to be about championships and wins and losses. It's going to be about things that have to do with the development of players—spiritual matters—how players are treated, whether they grow personally or not."

I believe Ron spoke the truth. I've had many former players, who are now successful in a variety of professions, say, "You know, some of the most important years of my life were the years I spent as a football player at Nebraska learning about perseverance and discipline and character." If there is any legacy, that is it. It isn't how many games or championships we won, even though we all cherish those milestones. Those former players influence their children, the kids they coach and the people they work with on a daily basis. If their years in the Cornhusker football program equipped them to pass on the values they learned here, that's all the legacy I could ever ask for.

A lot of coaches might view Nebraska's long streak of winning seasons as a legacy worth claiming, but I don't see it quite that way. Don't get me wrong—winning is great, and I will always be proud of the players and coaches who worked together with me to forge those championship teams.

But whatever legacy I leave is written on the hearts of the players I coached, through the way we treated them and in the values we promoted. I hope it is also written on some of the hearts of the people with whom I served on Capitol Hill, the people in my congressional district and the people who now work with me in Nebraska's athletic department. And I pray it will be written on the hearts of the children who are a part of the mentoring program, TeamMates. There is no way to calculate a win-loss record when it comes to them. There is only a determination to make a difference, one child at a time.

The best legacy any person can leave is an intact family with solid values and good character. I am very proud of my three children, my wife Nancy, our four grandchildren, and our two sons-in-law and daughter-in-law. They are what make life worthwhile.

LEADING

Leadership is communicating to people their worth and potential so clearly that they come to see it in themselves.

STEPHEN COVEY

What Makes a Good Leader?

There are effective leaders and there are ineffective leaders—and I've been both at one time and another. I think that one thing I've had going for me is that I have always tried to learn from my mistakes. I believe that this is an essential quality for anyone who desires to grow into effective leadership.

I have been in various leadership positions for many years, and that means I've had plenty of chances to make mistakes and learn from them. I have also had a lot of time to observe both effective and ineffective leaders at work and to learn from their mistakes and successes. One thing I have noticed: worldview and effective leadership are often linked. In the leadership courses I've taught over the years, I have tried to help my students make this connection because I think it is so important.

How a person leads is greatly influenced by his or her understanding of the world. Previously in the book, we looked at a few of the most prevalent worldviews at work in our culture. I believe that postmodernism, in particular, lacks the moral center needed for truly effective leadership. Leaders are called on each day to make decisions that affect the lives of many people, and those decisions must be based on a foundation more solid than feelings, opinion polls or personal preferences.

This is why I believe that worldviews are inextricably tied to leadership. As we explore the characteristics of several different kinds of leaders, keep this connection between worldview and leadership in mind.

Laissez-Faire Leaders

I believe there are three basic approaches to leadership. The first is a "laissez-faire" (hands-off) approach, which is, in a sense, an absence of leadership. You might say, "Well, that really isn't a type of leadership," but I would answer that there are a lot of people who have the title of "leader" but who really avoid leading. When they are pressed into making a decision, they often boycott their own leadership.

I saw this in politics quite often. For example, a governor who has pledged not to raise taxes may choose to defer to the state legislature when a severe economic crisis reduces tax revenues to the point that there is no option left but to raise taxes. The State Patrol, Medicaid recipients, schools, roads and other entities require state money and can't endure cuts beyond a certain point, so the governor forces the legislature to find ways to keep the state running, which means tax increases. The governor then vetoes these tax increases and keeps his pledge to his constituents, knowing full well that the legislature will have to override the veto and take the political hit. The point is, however, that someone has to decide which taxes to raise and by how much, how the revenues will be allocated, and which programs will be cut or streamlined. Laissez-faire leadership lets someone else make the tough decisions.

Laissez-faire political leaders are concerned about protecting their image at all costs, so you can never be sure where they stand on an issue. They take a poll, find out what people want to hear and then make decisions based on what will get votes or approval ratings. It's a popularity contest in which they seize on those things that seem to resonate with people—their hot buttons. They refuse to take a stand on the tough issues or only give a vague response when asked to comment on a particular concern, which allows them to straddle the fence.

As I mentioned previously, I was advised to develop a platform based on an opinion poll. I said, "No, I don't really need to take a poll to know what I'm all about. I'm going to tell people what I think needs to happen; what my vision is. If that doesn't resonate with them, then I'm not the guy they need."

I once knew a football coach who appointed offensive and defensive coordinators who made all the calls during a game. The head coach would never make a decision himself but would criticize the coordinators unmercifully if their calls didn't work. As a result, the coordinators were unwilling to take necessary risks and limited themselves to "safe" calls that were less likely to draw fire from the head coach.

Sometimes, you see leaders in business who are reluctant to tackle the tough issues. If there's something difficult or controversial, they make excuses about needing more information before they decide the correct course to take. They may appoint a committee and say, "Let's let the committee study these things and come back with a recommendation. Then we'll think about taking action based on what they say." They rarely say, "I believe that this is where the company needs to go, and we're going to begin making the tough decisions that are necessary to get us to that place." They simply put off making decisions, with the result that those who are under them are often left with no direction. Laissez-faire type leadership is much more prevalent than people think.

Transactional Leaders

The second approach to leadership is transactional leadership. This is the most common leadership style, in which the leader says, "If you do this for me, I'll do that for you. If you work overtime, you'll get paid extra. If you do a good job on this report, I'll give you more responsibility. If you do what I tell you to do and you're always on time and you work hard, I'll give you a raise." It's this for that, and it's traditionally how most people and companies conduct business. Transactional leaders reward good performance and punish bad performance; they focus on external outcomes such as turning a profit, passing grades or winning games.

Research indicates that, generally speaking, a system of reward works better than one that threatens punishment, but in transactional leadership both elements are present: "If you're late again, we're going to dock your pay. If you don't play well this week, you're going to go to the second team. If you don't get your expense report in by a certain date, your budget will be cut." If things get too negative, morale suffers.

Further, this model of leadership sometimes results in something I call "passive punishment." An example would be an employee thinking that he is doing a great job, when all of a sudden he gets a negative performance review. Nobody told him that there was a problem or that he needed to do anything differently, and now it's too late—it's in your file. Or maybe that woman in the cube across the hall from you gets fired. Nobody ever had a clue that anything was wrong; one day she's just gone, and everyone starts looking over their shoulder, wondering if they're next. This is why, when I was a coach, we graded our players on every play and reviewed game films and their grades before we announced any changes on the depth chart. We tried to keep them informed about how they were doing every step of the way.

A passive-punishment environment can be damaging to an organization. It fosters a poisonous culture that pits people against each other. Passive transactional leadership creates a culture of fear. At times, people lose their jobs, are demoted or must take a pay cut. If leaders are continually providing feedback on areas that need improvement or provide information regularly on market conditions that may result in layoffs or pay cuts, an organization can still function effectively. Negative episodes with no feedback or warning are destructive in any organization.

Transformational Leaders

Then there's a third style of leadership often referred to as transformational leadership, which some people call servant leadership. This type of leadership often springs from a Christian worldview. Jesus said that whoever wants to become great must become a servant of all (see Mark 10:43). Of course, servant leaders may come from other faiths and other worldviews. Whatever their background, however, they are not all that common.

Research shows that transformational leaders are often more effective, but that it is more difficult to be an effective transformational leader. They hope and plan for good external outcomes, but their effectiveness relies on adherence to principles and an ability to cultivate strong relationships, cohesiveness and a sense of common purpose rather than on extrinsic goals and rewards. Transformational business leaders focus on releasing creativity and innovation (which often leads to an increase in profits). Transformational teachers and mentors focus on helping students apply new knowledge to their lives (which often leads to excellent grades). Transformational coaches focus on building teams whose members trust each other and work together seamlessly (which often leads to a better win-loss record). But profits, good grades and wins are not the focus; they are a byproduct.

Early in my career, I was more of a transactional leader. I felt pressure to carry on the legacy begun by Bob Devaney, and focused my energies on the bottom line: winning football games.

I didn't *choose* transactional over transformational leadership—I didn't even know what those terms meant. I just focused on achieving the external outcome I wanted, and that focus led to a performance-based leadership style.

As time went on, however, and as I thought and read more about being a good leader, I realized that I had a choice. (John Wooden's books, and later Stephen Covey's work, helped to crystallize this choice in my mind.) I could continue serving the outcomes I desired, or I could choose to serve the people I was called to lead. Servant leadership is difficult because the leader is required to exemplify characteristics that are often rare:

1. The leader is willing to sacrifice self-interest for the good of the group.
2. The leader is willing to listen empathetically to understand followers.
3. The leader is a role model—exemplifies qualities that followers admire.
4. The leader is able to communicate and inspire others toward a shared vision.
5. The leader's actions are rooted in principles and values rather than external rewards.
6. The leader encourages growth, increased responsibility in followers.
7. The leader is dedicated to having his organization serve others and be a constructive force in society.

8. The leader has exceptional awareness and vision—can anticipate future trends and events.

My faith also played a role in changing the way I coached. I understood that Jesus calls His followers to be servants. I could see that the apostle Paul lived out this call to servanthood. Here was a man with enormous talent and charisma who had obviously been gifted with the ability to motivate and challenge people toward a goal. Yet Paul saw himself as a servant of the churches in which he ministered, willing to face incredible personal hardship on their behalf. He focused his energies on the wellbeing and continuing growth of the people under his care, confident that God would take care of the outcome.

Please don't get the idea that I was some kind of religious nut. I was simply trying to apply principles of faith in a highly competitive arena. We wanted to win, but we also wanted to do it according to principle. The desire to serve my players was rooted in my Christian faith, yet people of other faiths, such as Anwar Sadat, Nelson Mandela, and Mohandas Ghandi, were all exemplary servant leaders from other faiths.

Making the Change

It didn't happen all at once, but I began to shift my focus away from the outcomes I wanted and toward the people around me. I began to listen to and value their thoughts and opinions more. I tried to inspire and motivate rather than reward and punish. I spent more time with players in the weight room, at meals and after practice, and as I did I began to see them as valuable for who they were instead of for what they could do.

Making these kinds of connections took a lot of time because relationships are built one-on-one. As I became more connected with the coaching staff and the players, I felt more free to share my journey of faith.

As time went by, at the start of each new season, I gathered the whole team and staff together and briefly talked about where I was coming from philosophically and spiritually. There were no high-pressure tactics to get everyone to agree with me or to make some kind of spiritual commitment; I just wanted everyone to know that my beliefs were the driving force behind my leadership and decision-making. Since I would be making decisions that would affect their lives, I thought it was appropriate for me to let them know the philosophical genesis of most of those decisions. I'm sure that some players appreciated my openness, while others probably wondered what this had to do with football. However, I believed that the way people were treated had a lot to do with team chemistry, and that chemistry had a lot to do with football.

My last 10 years or so of coaching, I began to focus on hiring and mentoring coaches who also had a transformational approach to leadership. They didn't have to be Christians, but it was important to me that they have a strong spiritual center out of which came their ideas about how to treat players and create teams. I also wanted them to be positive role models for the young men in the program, people to look up to and admire. As I've mentioned, fatherlessness has had an enormous impact on many young people, and having strong and trustworthy role models can help to heal kids who have grown up without dads. Some days we were better role models than others, but we always cared about the players regardless of their level of contribution on the field.

One might get the impression that every leader neatly falls exclusively into one category or another. It has been my observation, however, that reality often doesn't match theory. The most decisive, hard-driving transactional leader may occasionally duck a hard decision by appointing a committee, thereby showing a laissez-faire streak. Someone who is mostly a servant leader occasionally has to administer reward and punishment. The person who ordinarily ducks decision-making like the plague may suddenly and decisively administer reward and punishment. Most leaders, most of the time, however, exhibit one style over another.

Accentuate the Positive

In the book *How Full Is Your Bucket*, Don Clifton and Tom Rath outline the tragedy that happened with American prisoners during the Korean War. The highest percentage of all recorded prisoner deaths occurred during this war, even though the prisoners were not tortured and were reasonably well fed.

The high death rate resulted primarily from the negative environment in which the POWs lived. They were rewarded if they informed on each other and if they confessed things they had done during their lifetime of which they were ashamed. Any news from home that was negative was quickly brought to them, but anything of a supportive or positive nature was kept from them. The negativism took a toll, and many prisoners lost their will to live and simply succumbed to despair. Thirty-eight percent of these POWs died.

Don Clifton, one of the authors of the book, was as an associate of mine in the Department of Educational Psychology at the University of Nebraska. Don formulated a new approach to psychology based on much of the research he had done. At the time I met Don back in the 1960s, psychology focused heavily on the study of animals as they were conditioned to behave in certain ways through reward and punishment. Psychology was also heavily oriented toward deviant behavior and the study of various mental illnesses.

Don reasoned that if we want exceptional behavior, we would benefit from studying those who perform exceptionally well. At one point, he was asked to develop a personality inventory that would help identify the very best insurance salesmen. Don studied the top producers in the insurance industry and tried to identify traits they shared in common. He also looked at those who were not successful in selling insurance and examined what traits they did not have in common with the top producers. From this research, Don began to formulate a theory that each of us is like a bucket and that each of us has a dipper. We can put positive messages and information into other people's buckets, or we can, through negativism, deplete the reservoir of positive self-image in the bucket of others. Even though this seems rather common sense and simple today, at the time it was almost totally outside the scope of conventional psychology.

Don observed that positive comments and feedback must outnumber negative interchanges in close personal relationships, such as between family members, by a ratio of at least 5 to 1. When the number of positive and negative interchanges began to approach 1 to 1, divorce and dysfunction were likely to follow. In the workplace, he noted that a 3 to 1 positive ratio was indicative of a cohesive, productive workplace; anything less than that percentage resulted in a great deal of negativism and dysfunction.

So, what does all this have to do with the high death rate of Korean War POWs? Well, Don reasoned that if bad news from home, informing on each other and a breakdown in the chain of command could have such terrible outcomes, then maybe the opposite behavior could create positive results. He believed that an environment that recognized and celebrated desired performance—one that emphasized praise rather than condemnation and one in which people worked together in a spirit of support and encouragement—would unleash creativity, energy and productivity.

I came to believe that catching a player doing something right and reinforcing it with praise was much more effective in shaping behavior than catching him doing something wrong and punishing him for it. Many times, people equate coaching with criticizing and punishing, and it is true that much coaching is of this nature. However, I don't believe it is as effective as providing a great deal of positive feedback.

I had lunch one day with the Commandant of the Marine Corps, General Charles Krulak. We were comparing basic training in the Marines with pre-season football training. General Krulak told me that the Corps had changed its approach to its new recruits: In times gone by, the point of basic training was to break down each recruit's will so that he or she would follow orders no matter what. But, he said, the focus now was on building teams.

Why? Because somewhere along the line, the Corps did its research and found that the reason Marines would go charging up a hill in the face of machine gun fire wasn't because they were trained to follow orders no matter what; the reason was that they cared so much for their fellow Marines, and they didn't want to let them down. In light of this new understanding, the Corps changed its approach to basic training to focus much more on building strong relationships among the Marines and forming cohesive teams.

So that's what they did. The Marine Corps trainers tried to catch trainees doing something right, and they found that rewarding good work got them further much faster than punishing mistakes and humiliating new recruits.

Unfortunately, there are still remnants of the old military basic training approach within coaching circles. Coaches perpetuate this practice because they were coached that way as young athletes and assume that this is the only effective way to coach. I once had a high school coach from Nebraska thank me for showing him and others that there was another way to achieve top performance. This coach won numerous state championships after abandoning some of his "old school" practices.

I tried to approach coaching players in the same way—catch them doing something right—and encouraged my staff to do the same. Instead of tearing a player down for doing something wrong, we emphasized what they were already doing right. "Tackle, you put your head up, locked your arms and drove your feet. That's a great example of what we're looking for." Even when correction was necessary, it was possible to do it in a positive way: "Tackle, I've seen you do it right a thousand times, and I know you can do this. You're doing great with your locked arms and your feet positioned, but you've got to keep your head up."

I made it clear to the coaching staff that there was no place for humiliating or dehumanizing players. On the rare occasion when one of the coaches got caught up in the heat of the moment (usually during a game) and began to berate a player, I'd try to remind him, "Don't just tell him what he did wrong—tell him how to do it right." A player who has made a mistake usually knows that he has made a mistake—he doesn't need someone to tell him, and he certainly doesn't need someone to tell him what a useless player and terrible human being he is. He needs someone to tell him how to fix it, and that's what a coach is for.

Our coaches were very positive for the most part. I recall the time Lou Holtz, who was then coaching at Arkansas, visited

Nebraska and watched us practice and sat in on our meetings. Before he left he told me that the one thing that most impressed him was how positive our coaches were and how little negativism or humiliation he observed. It was nice to have a coach of Lou's experience and stature pick up on that aspect of our program.

Focusing on the positive and trying to catch players doing something right did not mean that players never suffered consequences for poor behavior. But our policy was to punish poor behavior, not mistakes. If it was clear that a player was making a habit of giving less than full effort or was deliberately ignoring instructions, we put him on the bench. If he didn't go to class, we put him on the bench. But when we did so, we invested time and energy into finding out what was beneath the player's behavior. Was there something going on at home? Was he worried about his classes? Did he have a conflict with someone on the team? Sure, there were a handful of players over the years who were downright lazy or who had bad attitudes—but in my experience, the vast majority of people want to do the right thing and just need help doing it.

In the end, this approach to leadership and team building is related to my faith. I believe that each and every person should be treated with the dignity and respect that they deserve.

A Different Approach

When I first took over as head coach in 1973, it wasn't all a bed of roses, as I was coaching players who had been recruited by Bob Devaney and who had great loyalty and affection toward him. I was also working with coaches who had been hired by Bob, and most of them had been with him at the University of Wyoming. Some had even been with him when he was a high school coach in Michigan. As a result, I was the new guy on the block, and even though I had been an assistant at Nebraska, I'm sure that I was seen as someone who had not necessarily earned his spurs.

I probably wasn't as effective in regard to leadership during my first few years as head coach. In *Heart of a Husker*, edited by Mike Babcock, one player who was a senior my first year as head coach in 1973 wrote this: "It didn't feel the same with Coach Osborne as it did with Coach Devaney. And maybe, again, that was obviously a difference in personalities. It just was . . . Devaney was just different. He was more of a gambler, put it out on the line, and Tom was an *X*s-and-*O*s type of guy."

Another player pointed out that the players saw a contrast between the way I coached and the way Bob Devaney approached the game. That's the problem with following a famous coach—you aren't the former famous coach, and there is really nothing you can do to change that fact. The player said, "To try to follow Bob Devaney was really tough because everybody thought the world of him. He walked into a room and everybody just shut up. You didn't talk. We used to call him 'the old man.' And when he walked in, you didn't really say much because you just respected him so much."

This player also sensed the fact that there was dissatisfaction on the part of many fans. He said, "Tom was under a tremendous amount of pressure from the fans following Bob and having to try to meet expectations. People said, 'Hey, we shouldn't have lost this game. We shouldn't have lost that game.' I think we ended up 9-2-1 Tom's first year, and the year before we were about the same. But everybody was down on him, just because it was him."

Another player from 1973 said, "Tom was younger and didn't have the experience. I remember there were some pretty unhappy people when Tom got the job . . . I think part of the difficulty, and I don't think it's a whole lot different with probably any new coach, and especially a younger coach, was following a Bob Devaney . . . Well, Tom Osborne had a completely different personality than Bob. His idea of fun and Bob's were 180 degrees apart."

Some of the concerns expressed by the players who played for me in 1973 were due to the fact that I was not only different from Bob Devaney but was also serving as the offensive coordinator and head coach at the same time. This meant that I called the plays and was heavily engaged in *X*s and *O*s on every play. And then, part of it was also due to the fact that I was focused on the bottom line: winning games. Bob had been focused on winning also, but he had earned a high level of trust and confidence through years of successful coaching. I knew that I was never more than one bad year away from being fired. We won nine games, lost two, and tied one in 1973, which by most standards is a fairly good year. However, we lost to Oklahoma 27-0 in our last game of the regular season.

There was unrest among the players. My response to the embarrassing loss at Oklahoma was to work harder on the practice field. Some of the older players didn't like this, and things got a little tense; there was talk of a revolt. Eventually, everyone pulled together, and we prepared well. Had we not gone down and beaten Texas 19-3 in the Cotton Bowl at the end of the season, things would have really been rough around Lincoln. I would not have been fired, but the dissatisfaction would have been intense. It was fairly intense even with the Cotton Bowl win.

But things did get better. As the following quotes (taken from Mike Babcock's *Heart of a Husker*) indicate, much of what I mentioned previously in regard to transformational leadership did resonate with these players. I include it here as an example and encouragement for others who may want to lead in a transformational way.

Several players indicated they felt cared for and valued as people:

Isaiah ("I.M.") Hipp

Running Back, 1977-1979

I can still say Tom Osborne is a good friend. He cared in a way coaches don't normally do. He tried to put an emphasis on every person. Even if there were 101 players, he made an attempt to connect with everyone. He had a great ability to relate to people. The guidance and direction he gave me as a head coach and a man, as a person, stays with me. I believe that's the reason I am what I am today.

Turner Gill

Quarterback, 1981-1983

I thought Coach Osborne was very genuine. I knew he really cared about me as a person, even more than he did as a football player. Yes, he recognized me initially because of my football talents and all that, but I knew he cared about me deeply as a person. That meant a lot to me. I wanted to go somewhere where someone was going to help me become a better person through those four years of my life. I knew he was going to be able to do that for me, no matter what happened football-wise, baseball-wise, or whatever.

Tony Veland

Defensive Back, 1992-1995

I had a sense of trust [in Coach Osborne] early on. And I'll tell you what solidified it. I never thought negative of him, but what really made me respect him probably more than anything else was in the season when Lawrence Phillips was having all those troubles, when Coach Osborne suspended him and then brought him back. Obviously, Coach Osborne knew he was going to take a lot of flak for that. And he did take a lot of flak. But that meant a lot to me because it said, "Okay, consider Lawrence, consider his past and consider his future." If I were in that situation, would I want somebody to give me a chance? Would I want somebody to look after me? Or would I want somebody to close the book on me and write me off, send me back where I came from? When he gave Lawrence a chance, that really proved to me, really showed me, he cared about the individual first. He didn't care what everybody was going to say about him. He was that strong of a Christian. His convictions were strong. And he was looking out for our best interests. After that, I was really glad I made the decision to go to Nebraska.

Some indicated how important a positive environment was:

Kris Van Norman

Defensive Back, 1980-1982

It was pretty clear when he was unhappy. But he was always able to keep it in perspective and be constructive. You'll see some—a coach, a teacher, a boss—who will dress you down and never offer anything positive. Coach Osborne was always able to round the whole package out. If you were going to criticize somebody, tell him what he was doing wrong and then tell him what he needed to do differently to make it positive and constructive, not just a total destructive, diminishing comment . . .

Trev Alberts

Linebacker, 1990-1993

Coach Osborne fostered an environment. He didn't allow negativism. He didn't allow assistant coaches who were constantly at our throats. They demanded an awful lot, but I was never cursed at. I was never told how worthless I was. Coach Osborne and his assistants didn't coach out of fear. Ultimately, when it comes down to it, third-and-one and you've got to get off the field, or fourth-and-one at the end of a game, who are you going to play for: the person you've developed a genuine respect and love for, someone who cares about you and your family, or someone who just screams and yells at you?

Some commented on the importance of the process rather than focusing on the bottom line:

Tommie Frazier

1992-1995

For Coach Osborne, it's the journey. At first, it's hard to convince someone of that. But then you start realizing, "Hey, what he was saying was true. It is a journey. Everything is a journey. Life is a journey. Your destination is to make it to heaven. But you have to go through a journey in order for that to happen." The same thing is true in sports; everybody's goal is to win a championship. But there are games. The games are the journey; the workouts, the conditioning, and all that kind of stuff are the journey. The destination is to get to the championship. And if everything falls into place and you do everything you're supposed to do, you're going to reach your destination. That's what Coach Osborne taught.

Jon Hesse

Middle Linebacker, 1994-1996

There was one kid on the elevator, a freshman. It was probably four or five weeks into the season, maybe a little bit later, but the high school football season was still going on. This kid, he wasn't going to be there in a year or two, most likely. He was a walk-on wide receiver, I think, or a defensive back. I had no idea who he was because there were like 150 guys on the team. But Coach Osborne looked at this kid and said, "Hi, Jimmy," or whatever it was, calls him by his first name. I didn't know this kid's name, but Coach Osborne did and then he said, "Hey, how ya doing?" The kid was from some small town in Nebraska, and Coach Osborne said he saw where Jimmy's high school team had beaten its big rival. He gave that kid respect, made him feel important, not only acknowledged him and said his name, but also acknowledged his high school team had won a big game. The kid was right out of high school and that was still important to him. I take what he taught into my daily life now: It's about the journey. Championships, who cares? You want them, but they don't make you feel any different. So you'd better enjoy getting there and just doing things with excellence. If you're going to do it, let's do it as well as we can and at as high of a level as we can. . . .

Some players pointed out the importance of consistency:

Broderick Thomas

Defensive End, 1985-1988

When I look back, I had too much fire. I needed a guy like Tom. I needed a guy to calm me down, tell me it was going to be all right. My fuse was always short. I was ready to play at the drop of a hat. If the wind kicked up, I was ready. Tom was real calm. It was like they dropped me off on the moon until I talked to Tom or Charlie. It was rough at first, but all the things I went through just made me better.

Ed Stewart

Inside Linebacker, 1991-1994

I continue to be impressed about how long all of those coaches stayed together [at Nebraska] and how well they worked together. I'm sure they had their tiffs. They had different personalities and maybe everybody wasn't the best of friends. But you never would have known it, the way they handled themselves and the way they got along. Unity, working together, was so integral to our championship run. And it was evident that message came from the top down, that those guys were practicing what they were preaching. They were telling us to get along, play well together. You're taking all these people from different backgrounds, races and different levels of ability, getting them to buy into one vision and then work in concert to get something done. It was just phenomenal. And it's not easy to do.

Honesty was a key factor for both players and coaches:

Doug Glaser

Offensive Lineman, 1987-1989

For me, it came down to Nebraska, Oklahoma and Texas in recruiting. I just felt like Coach Osborne was the only one who was honest and truthful with me. He said, "Hey, if you can contribute for two years, you've been a success. And we're going to work hard on trying to get you a degree. I can't promise you any playing time." That wasn't the way the other recruiters were. Really, the two things about it were I trusted him; I felt like he was the only one shooting straight with me. And I wanted to go somewhere with a winning tradition, which Nebraska had.

Frank Solich

Assistant Coach, 1979-2003

I think Tom is an extremely organized person and really able to move through things in a timely fashion, so meetings and time spent together as a staff were always productive. He could make quick decisions but he took in the views and thoughts of his assistants, was open to ideas. He would measure those ideas very quickly and process them in a manner that enabled him to move forward. He was, and is, a man of his word. When he told you something, that was the way it was. You didn't have to worry about it, debate it. You knew his word was good. For a long time at Nebraska we didn't work with contracts. But no one felt uncomfortable about that. I don't know that he ever had a team that didn't believe in him, that didn't believe in the system and what we were doing. He would show his emotions at times. It would be under control, but you knew when he was upset, when he didn't feel you were playing to your ability. It came across. It didn't come across in a berating manner. It wasn't a screaming Tom Osborne you would get. But his feelings and emotions would show when things weren't going well.

One player even used the term "transformational":

Jamie Williams

Tight End, 1979-1982

He always seemed to be a man who was looking to the horizon. He had a vision. Tom Osborne defines leadership. Leadership, the field in which I have my doctorate, comes in a lot of different packages, but I think Tom encompasses what they call the transformational leader, the adaptive leader. He had his core style. But I watched him adapt, and when it was time for him to get on us and to prod us, he would do it. When it was time to encourage us and inspire us, he would do it. . . .

The following additional quotes were gathered for the publication of this book. Many of these quotes reflect themes of caring, process, honesty and consistency. Some of these quotes are from people I worked with in Congress, the athletic department, and TeamMates, and they mention the importance of listening, preparation, and operating on principle rather than opinion polls.

Jason Peter

Defensive Tackle, 1993-1995
(Currently a Lincoln, Nebraska, sports talk show host and author of the *New York Times* bestselling book *Hero of the Underground: My Journey Down to Heroin and Back*)

Coach Osborne as a leader can't be described with just one word. Perhaps his greatest impact on me was how he treated people. He never judged, wasn't swayed by what he thought fans might want nor pressured by the media. Instead, he always tried to do what was best for each person. He never made decisions so that his team would be better; rather, he made decisions so that each person could be the best person possible.

When it came to the staff and the players he encouraged everyone in the Nebraska football program to have the same qualities and characteristics as an actual family. He wanted everybody to know everybody else. The coaches knew the players' families; the players knew the coaches' families; the players knew the secretaries by name and the secretaries also knew our families by name. When you have that kind of family atmosphere, people form relationships that last and commitments that say, "I will do anything for you." That's how we were at Nebraska: Family. Coach Osborne was a father figure for a lot of us. Being away from home for the first time, things came up where we would want to sit and talk, and Coach Osborne always made himself available.

A leadership quality that I learned from Coach Osborne that I still practice today is preparation. Coach always wanted to be prepared for any scenario the opponent could throw at him. The teams I played on were so good because we worked harder than our opponents. Practices during the week were tougher than any game I played in on Saturday. If the team we were playing that week had a reputation of being physical then Coach Osborne made sure that we were very physical during practice. When Saturday would come the so-called physical team was completely outmatched. There was certainly a focus on out-working our opponent but to me that falls under preparation.

Bob Bettger

Agricultural Staff for Congressman Osborne in
Third Congressional District of Nebraska

Retired Farmer and Agricultural Liaison for the
Nebraska Department of Natural Resources

Tom Osborne's leadership style was thoughtful. He would study the issue at hand and make the best possible decision for the constituents and the State. He was decisive. He would take a position based on principle, logic or best long-term outcome where others would rather take a poll to see what was more popular at the moment. Tom Osborne's greatest impact, not only on me but on most people that know him, is how he leads by example. I believe that in every aspect of his life, personal, family, and business, people know his actions as a person and leader show compassion, respect and a moral and spiritual component.

Pat Logsdon

Associate Athletic Director for
Administration, Senior Woman Administrator,
University of Nebraska, Lincoln

It is clear that Coach Osborne has a goal of developing future leaders and building on the foundation of his leaders within the department. Individuals are not directed on how to accomplish a goal but are challenged to go do it and his support will be provided. He has an unbelievable trust in his staff. Coach Osborne is the epitome of a servant leader as is evidenced by the establishment of his TeamMates mentoring organization. He has a never-ending desire to make a difference in the lives of young people by helping them reach their full potential. Coach Osborne never deviates from his values and is passionate about always doing the right thing. He is a man of his word and believes that being brutally honest always pays off. He will do everything he can for his employees; thus he quickly earns the trust and respect of his followers who are willing to walk the plank for him because they know he will be first in line.

Jim Pillen

Former Player, TeamMates Board Member
CEO of Progressive Swine Technologies

Tom is a brilliant man with extraordinary gifts that at times I am not sure he really fully appreciates. He can study issues and know the details of any subject to a depth greater than many that would be very deep into it. An example would be when he became our district's congressman. He was able to get a better handle on farm policy and some of our problems and solutions than most of us who have been in the battle our entire life. He then uses his leadership skills to develop consensus and to get everyone to believe they can do more and in the end make things better. It doesn't matter if it was on our team or in the Third District getting people to understand and believe that we can take something on and be successful.

Tom is very consistent and fair. His 25 years of unparalleled success as head coach, what he accomplished as our congressman and what he is doing today as our AD attests to the impact his ability to bring people together, listen to them and help each of us do more then we ever thought possible as testament to his leadership results and style.

My greatest takeaway is that Tom believes in the daily process of life. He never once asked us to win a game. He pushed us to work as hard as possible to have an attitude to make ourselves better today then we were yesterday. If we took on this approach whatever the outcome we could live with ourselves and look each other in the eye. Whether it was a weekly process from game to game of a season, raising our families or our business I have found it to be a key pillar to life.

John Schuele

TeamMates Board of Directors
President of WaittCorp Investments LLC

Coach's leadership style is like no other I have seen. He is quiet and mild in manner, yet a great motivator. He is a skilled strategist and inspired visionary, yet has great command of all the details of any task or subject at hand. He makes you want to be better and to achieve great things individually, but more importantly, for the world and communities we live in.

It took a little while to warm up to his personality because he is soft spoken. Plus, when I first met him I was helping a young man trying to get recruited for a football scholarship, so we were on opposite sides of the fence so to speak—the young man's grades were not the greatest and there were some minor character flaws to discuss.

Coach is a great listener. My dad once told me after I graduated from college, the whole world talks and nobody listens; shut up and listen and you will learn a lot. I never met anyone who listens as much as Coach does. This makes him a great collaborator, a great decision maker and, finally, a great leader.

He has acted on suggestions and always keeps an open mind. He recently gave Vershan (my little from Big Brothers Big Sisters who is 34 years old now) a second chance to interview to work at the university despite a "checkered" past. He listened to why Vershan deserved a second chance (and he didn't have to) and consistent with Coach's history he also gave him a second chance to interview with Coach Pelini for a staff position. Tom Osborne models servant leadership in every action of his life every day because of how humble he is. Examples are hard to come by, but as the former treasurer of TeamMates, I know that Osborne's personal sacrifice financially has been humbling for me to witness. In addition, he always acts like a servant to the staff and volunteers of the TeamMates program. He will go to a three-hour fundraiser in Omaha, where he will sign autographs for hundreds of people (not to just make the fundraiser a success, but because he feels he owes every person his attention), then he will drive four to five hours, and the next morning be at a breakfast event in some other city.

Tom Osborne is a TeamMate mentor himself and was while he was a congressman. I mean, come on! Here is a guy who is a congressman, has many commitments the three days he is back in Nebraska each week, has 3 children, grandkids he wants to see, and he still mentors a child (and even meets with an ex-mentee who is in jail). It makes me laugh when people say they don't have time or are too busy to mentor.

Erin Duncan

Legislative Director for Congressman Tom Osborne

When I first joined Tom Osborne's staff, it was difficult to get used to his style in the office. We were essentially a group of strangers who suddenly had to work as a team and we were spread out between Washington and Nebraska. The first six months were extraordinarily stressful and difficult for all of us. We had to figure out how he worked and Tom had to figure out how we ticked. We were a staff of young women—average age probably 25—not a bunch of football coaches desperate for time with the Coach of the Century. For awhile it seemed like we spoke different languages, and we probably did. I can't really pinpoint the tipping point for when the staff gelled, but it just did, over time, and we became a very close-knit family. Tom became a touchstone for me over the six years I worked for him and his support really helped me through some difficult times personally.

Tom was incredibly supportive of our decisions as his staff and would trust our judgment. There were many situations in which we had to make decisions very quickly. Staff was allowed to negotiate with committees, for example, but sometimes we had to ask Tom to make a phone call to the leadership or a Committee Chairman to move something along. He would ask for an update on the legislation or issue, and pick up the phone and make a call. I always appreciated how much trust he put in me and how he al-

ways took my/our side on an issue, regardless of the situation. We are talking about legislative policy issues. He trusted that we had done our homework and had good intentions.

Tom set broad goals or came back from a visit in the district with an idea for a bill, but then let the staff figure out the best way to implement the action he wanted. He didn't care too much about the process, unless we needed him to get involved. It really gave even very young staff a lot of responsibility and confidence. He would ask for regular updates and occasionally offer suggestions, but he trusted the legislative staff to do our work and he would do his.

Tom was also true to his word, and I always admired that. He didn't bend on his core principles to be politically popular. For example, he gave the Nebraska State Education Association a commitment during his first campaign to not support private school vouchers and he kept that promise, despite intense pressure at times from the White House and Republican leadership to change his position.

I think Tom's trust in me gave me confidence to make decisions that were difficult and to help me trust myself more personally and professionally. And, frankly, it taught me a lot about celebrity. Celebrity is only important in how you use it—whether you use it to help people or not. Tom did that, and I really admire that he did. He could have endorsed some football shoe or something and made more money but he chose to do something that would make a difference in the lives of people.

Perhaps the greatest lesson I learned from Tom was to let others around you shine. The greatest testament to someone's leadership is how supportive and encouraging they are of others. Tom had absolutely no fear that I could tell. He might/we might/a bill might fail to pass, but we weren't failures. As my friend John used to say, "he went for two." (In the 1984 Orange Bowl.) And I guess that's the greatest lesson. When given an opportunity, trust your team, and go for it.

Most readers will realize that people will seldom make statements for publication that are highly negative, so the above quotes may be overly kind. Knowing those quoted as I do, however, I doubt that they would provide information that they knew to be false.

The main point of this discussion is that over time I did develop a more transformational leadership style and most who worked with me appreciated it. They felt valued, trusted and empowered and responded with a high level of performance. I am honored to have been given the chance to work with them.

Reading about this leadership style may lead one to believe that we ran a "soft" program because we were not big on profanity, denigration or harsh treatment. I often heard from fans that I was "too nice" to win the big one. However, few teams played harder, were more physical or gave greater effort than the University of Nebraska. Few congressional staffs worked harder than the staff I had, and hopefully few athletic departments will be more focused on excellence then our current department.

BECOMING A MENTOR

A good coach will make his players see what they can become rather than what they are.

Ara Parseghian

My First Mentor

In Homer's epic poem *The Odyssey*, Mentor was the name of an elderly friend of Odysseus, the main character of the poem. When Odysseus left to go on a 20-year journey to participate in the Trojan War, he asked Mentor to supervise the upbringing of his son, Telemachus. Mentor advised Telemachus, served as a role model and instructor, and prepared Telemachus for his mission in life as an adult. Mentor encouraged Telemachus and was with him every step of the way as he advanced from childhood to responsible adulthood. Obviously, Homer and the ancient Greeks had an understanding of how important it was to have an adult who could serve as an advocate and care about the child unconditionally.

Mentor's role with Telemachus resonates strongly with me, as my father left to participate in World War II in early 1942, shortly after the Japanese bombed Pearl Harbor. He was gone for more than four years, and I did not see him during that time. We only got an occasional letter from the battle front. It was a very stressful time for the whole nation, and for my mother and my family in particular.

My mother, brother (Jack) and I moved to St. Paul, Nebraska, a small town north of Grand Island, to live with my maternal grandparents until my father returned. I had an uncle, Virgil Welsh, who lived across the road from us. Even though I don't recall my father specifically asking Virgil to take charge of helping me develop as a young man, that is certainly the role that Virgil occupied. Virgil taught me to hunt, to fish and to swim. He was someone I admired greatly, and I looked forward to having him come home from work every day so we could either go out to the Loup River to fish for catfish, or run his trap lines in the winter, or hunt ducks and geese in the fall. Thank heaven for his interest in me and his guidance.

Those four-and-a-half years were painful. As a child, I can remember feeling inadequate and atypical because I was the only young person in my class at school who didn't have a father present. Because of this, I can relate to many of the young people in our country today who experience fatherlessness.

Planning for Cultural and Spiritual Revival

As I addressed earlier, I've seen a sea change in our culture during the last 40 odd years. The cultural and sexual "revolution" of the 1960s helped to overturn much of what we collectively valued: traditional family, sex within marriage, drug-free living, hard work and personal responsibility.

I witnessed this change firsthand in the lives of the student-athletes whom I coached. Some of these young men had trouble developing meaningful and lasting marriage relationships and had no idea how to be good parents. Some had a cavalier attitude about sex that was unhealthy and even dangerous. A few had experimented with illegal substances. Some had no idea how to take charge of their education and succeed through hard work and determination.

I admit that not all the changes I saw in them were negative—in times past, coaches expected players to do what they were told and never question any decision. But players coming up in the last 20 years tend to question authority more than was once customary. Of course, this isn't always a bad thing—after all, how can we expect our young men and women to learn to think critically and develop good judgment if we never tell them why we are asking them to do what they are doing?

Yet many of us in the United States are concerned about the cultural change we have experienced. We appear to be drifting badly, almost rudderless in a troubled sea. We need a cultural and a spiritual revival—a "great awakening" as we have had in centuries past—when we, as a nation, wake up to our cultural slide and turn ourselves around.

I recall once having a conversation with Congressman Frank Wolf from Virginia, in which Frank mentioned that he prayed daily for spiritual renewal in our country. I always viewed Frank as being an exceptional congressman, someone who truly cared about those who were suffering, whether it was in Darfur or in his district in Virginia or in the greater United States. He was someone with whom I shared not only similar views with but also someone with whom I collaborated on several pieces of legislation.

Both Frank and I are a little older now, and it has always been the case that the older generation thinks that things are sliding downhill as compared to when they were younger. However, I think there is enough objective data on the horizon to indicate that the United States has drifted from its spiritual moorings and that the fabric of our country is unraveling in many ways. Evidence of this can be seen in the latest economic crisis, which was brought on by excessive greed on the part of some individuals who were more concerned about lining their own pockets than with the welfare of the country. The ripple effect has been devastating. As a nation, we have become very materialistic, and sometimes our traditional value system has suffered in the process.

I see mentoring the next generation as an important part of the coming renewal. I believe that being a mentor is not only an investment in the life of one child but also an investment in the future of our nation. In the next few sections, I want to tell you three stories about mentoring that may seem unrelated at first glance. Each, however, plays a part in the birth of TeamMates, the mentoring program that Nancy and I began in 1991.

Grandfather and the Traveling Preacher

The first story is about my grandfather, who grew up in western Nebraska near the small community of Bayard in the 1890s. His father was a veteran of the Civil War and an alcoholic who did his best, such as it was, to raise four kids on a small homestead. My grandfather didn't have much going for him, but at a pivotal point in his young life he met a traveling preacher named Currens, who saw his potential. Currens was most likely a circuit rider who traveled on horseback preaching in several communities. Currens encouraged my grandfather to go to college and become a preacher. At that time in our nation's history, very few people attended college, and the chances of someone from my grandfather's station in life going to college were just about zero.

Based on the affirmation my grandfather received from this man he admired, he caught a vision for his life that he might not have dreamed on his own. He scraped together enough money to ride the stagecoach about 60 miles to Alliance, Nebraska. From Alliance, he rode the train another 300 miles to Hastings, where he enrolled in Hastings College. He worked his way through school, became the captain of the football team in 1900, and eventually learned six languages, including Sioux. He also worked as a cowboy and at a trading post. After graduating, he attended seminary and became a well-known preacher. Eventually, my grandfather became a Nebraska state legislator.

My grandfather was killed by lightning when I was only eight or nine years old. As I grew up, I often thought of him. I wondered if my actions were pleasing to him, as I could imagine him observing me from heaven. This prospect made me uncomfortable on those days when I didn't find myself measuring up as well as I should have.

Because someone believed in my grandfather and, at a critical time in his life, imparted a vision of what he could achieve, he lived a full and successful life. Not only that, he made it his mission to impart that same kind of vision to his own children. During the Great Depression, living only on a meager preacher's salary, my grandfather saw to it that all five of his children went to college. Currens's impact on my grandfather's life was like a pebble thrown into a still pool of water: The resulting ripples have been felt in succeeding generations—from my father to me and, I pray, to my children and grandchildren.

Mentoring in the Dorm

The second story is one I alluded to previously in this book. When I asked Bob Devaney if I could join his coaching staff, he told me that he had no positions open. However, he said that if I wanted to do so, I could move into an undergraduate dorm with seven or eight players who were causing trouble. If I had success with them, Bob and I would revisit the possibility of coaching. These guys had developed a kind of frontier mentality: Anyone who trespassed their territory would suffer the consequences. The dorm counselors were afraid of them, and the school's administrators seemed at a loss for how to deal with the problem.

I took Bob up on his offer and moved in with the players—and it soon became clear to me why the dorm counselors had basically thrown up their hands and given up. The guys drank on occasion, which sometimes led to fights. I had to break up a couple of late-night brawls. Each time, I tried to make it clear that I represented Coach Devaney, and that if they didn't shape up, they wouldn't be around to play football. One young man was about to be expelled for throwing a snowball in the dorm and for stealing a newspaper. I appeared at a hearing on his behalf and convinced the authorities that he had some good qualities and deserved another chance. He went on to become an All-American lineman and was quite successful after leaving Nebraska.

When I wasn't breaking up fights, I made every effort to get to know each one of the guys. Living side by side with them, day in and day out, helped me to build relationships of trust. And that was the key, I think, in helping them turn things around. As time went on, their behavior mellowed out, the drinking decreased and their grades started to improve. Today, one of them is an English professor, one is an author, a couple are successful businessmen, one is a college coach and one owns a funeral home in Ohio. I'm glad that Coach Devaney did not give up on those young men. They needed some guidance, support and an occasional dose of discipline to show them how to make better decisions.

Eugene Lang

The third story concerns an evening in 1991. I had just come home from football practice, and when I walked through the door, Nancy shared that she had just watched a *60 Minutes* interview with a man named Eugene Lang. Mr. Lang had grown up in Harlem in New York City, founded a technology development company in the 1950s and then made quite a bit of money.

As a successful businessman, he was invited to speak at a sixth-grade graduation ceremony at the Harlem elementary school he had attended. While there, the principal told him that three-quarters of the students were unlikely to graduate from high school. In a moment of inspiration, Mr. Lang promised every sixth-grader full college tuition if he or she would stay in school through high school graduation. The I Have a Dream Foundation was born, and nearly 30 years later, Mr. Lang's scholarship promise to those sixth-graders has been repeated to more than 15,000 students in similar difficult economic circumstances.[1]

Nancy was so impressed with and inspired by Mr. Lang's commitment to young people that she asked, "What can we do?"

As I considered the question, I reflected on how things had changed in the 20 or so years since I began coaching. The out-of-wedlock birthrate had skyrocketed. Drugs and gangs had swept into neighborhoods across the country, even in the Midwest. The percentage of young people growing up without both biological parents had more than quadrupled.

It struck me, as I thought about all these things, that Nebraska's football team had enormous potential to make a difference in our community. With around 150 players who were greatly admired in our state, we might be able to make a difference in the lives of young people at a crucial time in their development.

The following day, I gathered the team together and said, "The guidance counselors in Lincoln's public schools think that students would benefit from some kind of mentoring. How many of you are willing to spend some time with a seventh- or eighth-grade boy?" Twenty-two football players raised their hands to volunteer, and they were soon matched with 22 junior-high boys.

When we first began, the guidelines were simple: Mentors were to meet with their "mentees" at least once a week. They could do things like visit the boys at school, bring them to practice, go to a movie or help them study. We also organized a monthly activity to do together—we ate pizza, played basketball, listened to a speaker or discussed goals and how to reach them.

Although things seemed to be going well, it wasn't long before I realized that the students were getting older and nearing a time when some of them might choose to drop out of school. With Eugene Lang in mind, we set up a meeting with all of the student mentees, their mentors and many parents. I made a promise that if the students stayed in school and out of trouble, we would see to it that they could go to college.

At the time, I didn't know where we would find the money, but I felt confident that we could raise it somehow. I began to think and pray about how to fund the boys' college educations, and it wasn't long before an interesting scenario presented itself. A Nebraska alumnus had done the math and figured out that I had recently led the football team to 100 wins, an achievement that Bob Devaney had also reached before his retirement. The university decided to throw a "Double 100" celebration to mark the occasion.

People's generosity overflowed, and we raised more than $200,000 dollars. We put the money in the University of Nebraska Foundation, where it could continue to increase until the day it was needed to pay for the students' college educations.

A few more years went by, and 21 of the original 22 students graduated from high school. Of those, 18 chose to attend college.

The stories of two of those young men are particularly well-known to me. One was a rather small blond-headed seventh-grader named Sean Applegate. Sean later played football for Lincoln High School and asked me during his senior year if he could come out for the Huskers as a walk-on the next year. He wasn't very big, but he had a solid record as a high-school player, so I agreed—and Sean exceeded all expectations. He eventually became a starter on the team and earned a football scholarship, which helped him graduate with a degree in Industrial Technology. Today, Sean is a teacher and is doing well. He also has served as a TeamMates mentor.

The second student was a born entertainer, a dread-locked young man named Eddie Brown. Eddie came to the University of Nebraska and made a name for himself as a musician on campus. He performed with the Scarlet & Cream Singers and eventually won a post-graduate scholarship to study at Oxford. Eddie now lives in Lincoln and heads the Eddie Brown Insurance Agency. He has done exceptionally well in the business community and has also chosen to be a mentor himself.

What Is a Mentor?

I share these success stories to emphasize the major impact that mentoring can have on our communities—and in the long run, our society as a whole. But what exactly is mentoring, and why is it so effective?

Mentoring is an investment in one person's life that pays dividends in the lives of many. I believe that a mentor makes three basic contributions to the life of a young person.

As my grandfather's story demonstrates, vision is the first contribution a mentor can make to a mentee's life. The traveling preacher, Currens, painted a picture of the future that my grandfather had not dared to imagine for himself. So many young people grow up in a similar situation, lacking a vision for what is possible in their lives. They may have never seen a person in their immediate family graduate from college (or sometimes even high school). They may have grown up without a father. Their knowledge about how to apply for college or technical school may be very limited. A mentor can help them imagine a successful future and can guide them through the process of making the right choices along the way.

Second, a mentor shows his or her mentee unconditional care. In its original language, the Bible calls this kind of sacrificial love *agape*, which is positive regard without conditions. It's not a warm fuzzy feeling but an unwavering commitment to another person. This is particularly important when we consider how difficult relationships with teenagers can be. Mentors don't always feel warmth and affection for their mentees during the adolescent years. Nevertheless, good mentors choose to treat their mentees with respect and care, and this kind of consistent love from an adult can be extraordinarily powerful in the life of a young person. We can will the best possible outcome for their lives irrespective of our emotions. Many teens find the effect of unconditional love to be transformational.

I'm probably not known as the most warm and fuzzy person in the world. When you're a football coach, you have to deal with people getting hurt. A lot. You can't spend too much time during a ballgame sympathizing with players' injuries; you have to be a general, so to speak, concerned with the next skirmish on the battlefield. It doesn't mean that you don't care, and I hope the players I coached knew that I cared a great deal—I tried, anyway, to express my care and concern on and off the field by being consistent and available. I've tried to do the same with the young men I have mentored through the years as part of my commitment to TeamMates.

The third contribution a mentor can make to the life of a young person is affirmation. Many youth do not receive much positive feedback, and it is difficult to achieve when they do not feel valued. Having someone who believes that they can accomplish great things is a powerful catalyst for achievement.

One of the things we tell our volunteer mentors is to find their mentee's strength. What does that young person do well? Conventional wisdom says that the way to be successful is to identify your weaknesses and then shore those up. But a lot of recent research indicates that truly successful and satisfied people concentrate on maximizing their strengths rather than trying to improve their shortcomings.

We try to apply this principle to mentoring by encouraging mentors to identify their student-mentee's strengths. Does he have musical or athletic ability? Is she strong in science and math? Does he have natural abilities with mechanics or electronics? Is she a good communicator? Whatever the strength, find it and affirm it. Reinforce it. Encourage it. Connect that strength with an extracurricular activity that will help the student to hone their talent and will help him or her succeed in college. (Generally speaking, the best predictor of college success is involvement in extracurricular activities.)

I saw the necessity of affirmation very clearly in athletics. When we affirmed a young player and expressed our belief that he could accomplish great things and be a major contributor to the team, he often grew into exactly that kind of athlete. If, on the other hand, a player was given very little encouragement and little hope that he could become a great player and contributor, his playing often deteriorated—a self-fulfilling prophecy, if you will. That's why we always tried, as a coaching staff, to be as positive as possible to each and every player. Coaching at its best is a form of mentoring because coaches are in a position to cast a vision, to care unconditionally and to give affirmation to players.

The Importance of Mentoring

Kim Baxter, a doctor who lives in North Platte, Nebraska, was mentoring a young man a few years ago who was in the eighth grade. Kim had been mentoring the young man for the better part of a year, but was somewhat discouraged in that it didn't seem that he was making much headway with the young man. The mentee didn't seem to have anything that interested him or motivated him.

Finally, Kim hit on the idea of teaching the young man how to play the guitar. The mentee had not been doing very well in school, so Kim brought his old guitar to school and told the young man that if his grades improved, he could take the guitar home and practice with it. This was the first thing that had sparked any interest during their mentoring relationship.

The young man's grades did get better; however, toward the end of the school year, his grades fell off a cliff. Kim was really discouraged. He had a conversation with the young man and indicated that he didn't think he was doing him any good as a mentor. Kim placed the blame on himself and told that young man that it wasn't his fault—he just thought that possibly someone else could do a better job of mentoring him. Kim also mentioned that since the young man's grades had fallen off, he thought it was only fair that the young man return the guitar. The young man dropped the guitar off at Kim's office one day, and Kim took it home. As far as Kim was concerned, their mentoring relationship was over.

The guitar Kim had given the young man was an old one that he normally never used. However, a couple of months later, Kim was going on a camping trip and thought that he would take along the old guitar—the one he had loaned to the young man—

as he didn't want his good guitar to get scratched or damaged. Prior to leaving on the trip he opened up the guitar case, and a note fell out. The note reads as follows: "I just want to thank you for your friendship and the time you have taken to meet with me. If you would be willing to still be my mentor, I promise to try harder in school. Please don't give up on me." When I read that quote it still brings tears to my eyes. That young man, like so many other young people, desperately needed an adult in his life who would care about him and would be unwavering in his commitment.

Kim mentioned that it was somewhat providential he ever decided to use the old guitar again, because there had been times when he had gone several years without playing it. Naturally, when he read the note, he realized that much more had been going on in the mentoring relationship than he had ever suspected. The young man had not even shown any particular emotion when Kim had told him that he thought he needed another mentor and that Kim would no longer be mentoring him. Obviously, the note indicated otherwise.

Kim immediately picked up the phone and called the young man to reestablish contact. Eventually the mentee did graduate from high school, and today he is pursuing a career as a mechanic and has done well with his life.

This story illustrates how important having an adult who cares for a young person unconditionally can be in that young person's life. Even though on the surface it may seem that nothing much is happening, mentoring can still be a very powerful influence in a young person's life. Kim serves on our TeamMates Board, and even though he is tremendously busy, he finds time to mentor. It is people like Kim who are making a huge difference in the lives of young people.

Mentoring in TeamMates

Sometimes, mentors who have been recruited into TeamMates are at first confused about what they are there to do. They think that being a mentor is, essentially, being a tutor—helping a young person with his or her studies. While our mentors do sometimes assist mentees with their homework, the primary objective it to build a relationship of trust in which they can impart a vision, care unconditionally and give affirmation to the student they are assigned to mentor. This can only happen when the mentor is committed and consistent.

We have found that if a mentor meets with their mentee at least 24 or more times during a 35-week school year, a positive relationship characterized by high levels of trust is the result, and their influence has a great impact on that child's future. If the mentor only shows up four or five times, however, the result is more damaging than if the relationship had never been established. The youth may feel that he or she is not important enough to warrant an adult's attention and investment. Needless to say, we try to be as clear as possible with our volunteer mentors about the importance of showing up.

Most of TeamMates's volunteers say that they receive as much as or more than their mentee from the mentoring relationship. This has certainly been my experience as a mentor.

I have been a mentor to three young men over the last 12 years. The first, with whom I started in 1997, was a seventh-grader who came from a large and sometimes difficult family situation. His father was deceased. He had experienced some run-ins with the law, and I visited him in an alternative school and later at a detention center. By some measures, I guess, I wasn't very successful. Not long ago, though, he called to let me know that he had earned his GED and is working two jobs to support his young child, of whom he is very proud. He told me that his goal is to be a great father, and I told him how proud I was of his decision. I went to his child's first birthday party at his fiancée's invitation and was blessed to see how this young man had grown into a responsible and caring adult. Seeing him reaffirmed to me that no one is ever beyond hope, and everyone should be given a shot at redemption.

My second mentee was in ninth grade when we began to meet together. He graduated from high school and eventually enlisted in the Marine Corps. He spent some time in Iraq and is serving our country with distinction.

I'm currently mentoring a bright young man in the fifth grade who has great potential. We have been meeting together for more than a year, and in that time, he has improved his academic performance significantly. We have an excellent relationship, and I look forward to seeing him each week.

We try to start TeamMates mentoring relationships in the fourth or fifth grade, because it is easier for mentors to create a bond with youth and establish positive patterns at an earlier age. It's never too late, but we believe that the earlier, the better. We also try to recruit mentors who will stick by their mentee through high school graduation. Not everyone can make that kind of years-long commitment, but that's the goal: a consistent, dependable and trustworthy relationship that the student knows will see him or her through graduation.

Investments in the Future

Not long after the Double-100 event at which we raised some money for TeamMates, I approached one of Nebraska's U.S. senators, Bob Kerrey, to tell him my vision for a mentoring program in our state. Bob was able to get a million-dollar federal grant, which was a huge shot in the arm for the program.

This federal grant was what is known as an "earmark." As mentioned earlier, earmarks have received a bad name in many circles; however, if the earmark use is clearly articulated and if the person requesting the earmark is identified, I believe that some earmarks serve the public well. I am confident that this federal money has already been returned to taxpayers many times over in reduced social costs due to incarceration, substance abuse, teen pregnancy and kids dropping out of school.

We expanded from mentoring only young men to also mentoring young women in the Lincoln public schools. We invited adults in the community to volunteer as mentors, in addition to the football players who were already a part of the program. From there, it didn't take long for TeamMates to spread across the state.

In every school with a TeamMates program, there is a building coordinator who arranges places for mentors and mentees to meet on a weekly basis. Actually, the building coordinator is the person in charge of matching mentors with students who have similar interests. Men mentor young men and women mentor young women and young men. We do background and criminal checks on all our volunteers and train them before they get started, and then host support groups so that mentors can share ideas and struggles.

As of Spring 2009, we had programs in 112 communities, mentoring close to 4,000 young people. Through data collection, we have found that 85 percent of our mentees show significant improvement in school attendance. This is a very significant statistic, as the best predictor of whether a student will drop out of school is absenteeism. Those who miss large amounts of school not only fail to learn but also often leave school without a high school diploma.

We also found that 75 percent of our mentees show a considerable decrease in discipline referrals, and 44 percent show noteworthy academic improvement. The decline in discipline referrals is important not only for the mentee but also for other students in the classroom and the teacher. A few disruptive students can create a chaotic learning environment for everyone. National research on mentoring also points to a decline in substance abuse, teen pregnancy, criminal behavior in mentees and improvement in relations with their parents and fellow students.

We are encouraged by the impact of TeamMates and have expanded beyond Nebraska's public schools. We are mentoring in parochial schools now, and we have four programs in Iowa and are planning to reach out to other states. Our goals are to mentor 5,000 students in the Midwest by 2010 and match 10,000 students with mentors by 2015.

TeamMates's funding comes from a variety of sources, including private donations, foundation grants, fundraisers and federal grants. Various TeamMates schools have applied for and won grants from the government and from philanthropic organizations. People in local communities believe in their programs so strongly that they are willing to do the hard work of organizing fundraisers to provide scholarships for TeamMates graduates. They have also been successful in receiving significant grant funding.

Mentoring for Success

When I went to Washington as a congressman, I served on the Agricultural Committee (because Nebraska's Third District is primarily rural) and on the House Committee on Education and the Workforce. I wanted this latter position because of my background in education and because education is something I'm very passionate about. That committee wrote No Child Left Behind (NCLB), which has since become a piece of legislation that many people have strong feelings for or against. I was able to get two amendments added to NCLB, which remained in the bill through its being signed into law by President Bush.

One of those amendments was called Mentoring for Success, which has been discussed previously. In the years since No Child Left Behind passed in Congress and became law, Mentoring for Success has been funded to the tune of 250 to 300 million dollars and has resulted in several hundred thousand mentoring relationships being established. In the end, that amendment may prove to have the most lasting and far-reaching impact of anything I did in Washington.

I have always thought that coaching is an important part of the teaching profession and that teaching at its best is mentoring. During all the years that I coached, the most satisfying aspect was not the wins or the championships but the opportunity to make a difference in the lives of the players with whom I worked. Athletics is always an emotionally charged experience. Student-athletes are much more ego-involved than students sitting in a history or mathematics class. They pay close attention to what is said to them, as their sense of self-worth is on the line.

There are so many teachable moments in athletics, and those moments are never more prominent than when adversity strikes. It may involve an injury to a player, a difficult loss, or poor performance at a critical time. How the coach responds at that time has a great bearing on the self-image of the student-athlete and whether they are able to learn from the adversity or whether they allow the adversity to overwhelm them.

I enjoyed my few short years in the classroom as well, but I can honestly say that the opportunity to teach young people through the sport of football was quite likely the most significant thing that I have done in my lifetime. Hopefully, I was a good mentor to them.

Note

1. "About Us: History" at IHaveADreamFoundation.org. http://www.ihaveadreamfoundation.org/html/history.htm (accessed May 2009).

FISHING, FLYING AND FAMILY

There is no doubt that it is around the family and the home that all the greatest virtues, the most dominating virtues of human society, are created, strengthened and maintained.

WINSTON CHURCHILL

A Lifelong Fisherman

I'm not sure exactly where my love of fishing came from, but I know it started very early in my life. One of the first memories I have of fishing was going out to a pond near St. Paul, Nebraska, with my uncle Virgil. My dad had gone off to fight World War II, and I must have been about five years old.

Virgil and I were fishing with bobbers and worms for bait and trying to catch bluegills and bass. He kept warning me that the grass on the pond's edge had grown out over the edge of the water and that I shouldn't get too close to the edge or would fall in. As most five-year-olds might do, I didn't pay a whole lot of attention and eventually stepped on the overhanging grass and fell in. There was a very steep drop off, and I kept going down and down. Virgil had turned away, heard the splash and turned around and saw my hat floating on the water. Fortunately, he was able to reach down under the hat and grab hold of my shirt and pull me out. I was totally soaked and somewhat cold, so that ended our fishing for the day, but that remains with me as my first memory of a fishing trip.

About four years later, shortly after my dad had returned from World War II, I was visiting at my grandparents' home on a Sunday in St. Paul and talked my uncle into taking me fishing on a cold, drizzly 40-degree day in March. I could tell that he didn't think we would catch anything and that it would be a waste of time. However, we still went and fished off of the bridge in the North Loup River without much success for about an hour. Then suddenly something grabbed the bait and took off. I could tell that this was not a little fish.

What ensued was a long struggle with a good-sized catfish, and eventually we were able to pull it in. I was so impressed with that fish that we wrapped it in newspapers and I took it back to our home in Hastings, where I eventually had a picture taken of it that appeared in the *Hastings Tribune.* I think that catch sealed it for me. I was a dyed-in-the-wool fisherman from that point on for the rest of my life.

I can also remember the first and only family vacation that we took. Shortly after my dad had returned from World War II, we went to the mountains with my grandparents. I remember driving past one trout stream after another and not being allowed to get out and fish, as this was primarily a sightseeing vacation. Finally, one day when we were driving through the Big Horn Mountains in Wyoming, I prevailed upon my dad to stop the car near a pretty trout stream. I floated a worm through a hole behind a rock and caught a trout that was probably six or seven inches long.

This was the first trout that I had caught; for some reason, trout had always captured my imagination as being the ultimate fish to catch. I can remember being very proud and my grandmother said, "There, Tommy, you have now caught your fish so we don't need to do this anymore." Of course, catching the fish simply whetted my appetite for more fishing, so it was an agonizing trip, seeing all of that great trout water and not having many opportunities to fish.

Even though my dad was not interested in fishing, I still managed to sustain my passion for fishing because my mom would occasionally get up early in the morning and drive me to a small stream 25 miles south of Hastings named Elm Creek. Each year there were a few trout stocked in Elm Creek, and I thought it was a great day if I managed to catch a couple of small trout early in the morning before I went to school.

Not an Outdoorswoman

It was only natural that I might assume that the person I would marry would share my interest in fishing. During our courtship, I raised the issue on occasion with Nancy and got the impression that she would enjoy doing some fishing once we got married. Nancy has somewhat different memories of these conversations and claims that I was never given any encouragement about her becoming a fisherwoman.

Whatever the case, as we planned our honeymoon, I incorporated some fishing, and have never heard the end of it. We were married at Nancy's home church, a Baptist Church in Holdrege, Nebraska, and drove to San Francisco. I had always thought that San Francisco was a beautiful city and thought that Nancy would enjoy some time there. She seemed to enjoy San Francisco but also was homesick, so it wasn't long before we started back toward Nebraska. I had planned a fishing expedition or two for the return trip, and this is where things began to fall apart.

We had agreed before our marriage that we would spend some time in Steamboat Springs, Colorado, which at that time was a small, sleepy town in western Colorado where Nancy had some relatives. Also there was excellent trout fishing. I had bought a pair of hip boots for Nancy and a small fishing rod, and I was sure that she would be thrilled with the trout fishing around Steamboat Springs.

Before you can go fishing, you have to have some bait, so the night before we were to go fishing, we went out to the city park with a cattle prod and proceeded to collect some nightcrawlers. The way this is done is to stick the cattle prod, which contains an electrical charge, into the ground. This makes things very uncomfortable for nightcrawlers, and it isn't long before they come squirting out of the ground. We had spent about an hour collecting worms, and I thought it was interesting and enjoyable (especially when I'd get hold of a crawler just when it tried to slither back into the ground. Playing tug of war with a worm is surprisingly entertaining). Nancy didn't say much about this activity, so I thought that the proceedings had been okay with her. The next day, however, I began to gain a little better understanding of how Nancy was perceiving the whole operation. We drove high in the mountains that day and took two of her small nephews with us to a place called Fish Creek Reservoir.

Nancy's nephews and I began to fish in earnest. Nancy had said that she would be right along, but after awhile, I began to wonder where in the world she went. I waited. And she still didn't catch up. Eventually, I trekked back the way we had come and found my new wife: Nancy had laid out a nightcrawler across a stone and was trying to stab it with the hook, which she had wrapped in a Kleenex.

This was a moment of truth for me, in which I realized that Nancy might not be an instinctive fisherwoman and our married life might not be quite what I had envisioned that it would be.

Three years later, we were back in Steamboat Springs, and Nancy's uncle Don took us high in the mountains on a very, very rough road back to a beautiful mountain lake called Luna Lake. Nancy was about seven months pregnant at the time. We hadn't been there very long before it began to rain. Don thought that we should head back, as there was a very steep incline that we had to climb in the Jeep. He knew that if the trail was sufficiently wet, we would never make it. Sure enough, as we tried to climb out of Windy Gap, we kept sliding backwards and eventually had to abandon the Jeep. We walked out roughly 10 miles to the nearest road, where we eventually caught a ride back into town. This was not long before our son, Mike, was born and probably didn't make Nancy's views on fishing any more endearing.

But I wasn't ready to give up yet.

A few years later, Nancy, our children and I went to Alamosa, Colorado, for a Fellowship of Christian Athletes camp. After an uplifting week, I thought it might be nice to tent-camp in the mountains for a few days. We bought a tent and went quite a ways back into the mountains, pitching the tent by a lovely little stream full of brook trout.

I thought it was heaven. Nancy slept with a hatchet next to her. It turned out that she was terrified of bears, which I'd never known. We spent one nearly sleepless night and that was the end of our camping adventure.

Several years later Nancy, my daughter Suzanne and I were in Idaho near the Teton Mountains. I talked Nancy and Suzi into hiking into a fairly remote stream. Someone at a fly shop whom we asked for directions had told us that this area had many grizzly bears. We slid most of the way down to the canyon floor where the stream was. I started fishing immediately and caught a couple of fish while Nancy and Suzi talked—mostly about what we should do if a bear came along. The more they talked, the more convinced they became that a bear attack was imminent. Within 20 minutes, they had me climbing up out of that canyon to "safety." Nancy hadn't changed her mind about bears. I have had several experiences in close proximity with grizzlies in Alaska while fishing for salmon—it was probably best that Nancy didn't go on those trips.

We had a small cabin for many years out on Lake McConaughy in western Nebraska. It was a beautiful spot, and the lake had trout that got to be pretty good size—up to eight pounds if I was lucky—and on a good day I could catch three or four of them. To catch them, though, I had to troll in the boat, and that meant somebody had to come with me to drive while I set the line and ran the downriggers. Nancy or one of the kids would occasionally agree to chauffeur me around the lake, which is 22 miles long and has its share of mosquitoes and flies, but as time went on, it got harder and harder to convince any of them to get up before dawn and come with me. It got to the point where not even our little dog, Ralph, would get in the boat with me. So, I was on my own when it came to trolling.

Although my children didn't enjoy trolling in my boat with me, sometimes for hours on end, they did occasionally go fishing with me. By the time my son, Mike, was 10 years old, he had caught a walleye of approximately 11 pounds, a rainbow trout that weighed about 7 pounds, and a striped bass that weighed 14 pounds. Maybe he had so much fishing success early that he lost interest in it. Today he prefers golf to fishing, although he will occasionally wet a line.

My daughter Ann would go out with me when we were casting for walleyes. She hated trolling, but enjoyed casting. I remember one evening we were fishing for walleyes on Lake McConaughy and the storm clouds started moving in. There was some electricity in the air and I remember that Ann's finger started to glow as she was casting her line. Apparently there was so much static electricity in the air that it lit up her finger. I decided at that point that it would be wise to get off the water fairly quickly.

My youngest daughter, Suzanne, is the one who is the most avid fisherman. She loves fly-fishing and is about as good as any fly-fisherman around. All in all, however, the intensity with which I fish has probably not been conducive to having children who are terribly passionate about fishing because of all the time that we spent in that boat trolling for trout on Lake McConaughy.

Nancy had become somewhat leery of going on fishing trips with me, but she would go if we had another couple or two to accompany us so that she had someone to talk to while I was out fishing. We went to Costa Rica a few years ago with two other couples who are good friends of ours, the Scotts and the Yanneys. I had read something about a fishing camp in the jungle on the west side of Costa Rica that looked intriguing. The tarpon fishing and snook fishing was supposed to be outstanding there, and I convinced the group that this would be a great destination. So we took off out of San Jose, the capital of Costa Rica, in two small airplanes, heading for a jungle airstrip.

For some reason, the men jumped on one plane and the three women on the other. The men's flight was relatively short and without incident, but we we waited and waited at the landing strip for the women's plane to arrive. Finally, two hours later, they landed. It turned out that as they had taxied out to the runway, they found that one of the doors on the small plane would not latch and they had to go back to the hangar to get it fixed. Then, as they taxied out again, the plane had a flat tire, and they had to go back and get that fixed before they could finally take off. The three women did not see this as an auspicious start.

As we moved into our cabins that evening, we noted that there was a fair amount of rustling in the walls. We couldn't figure out what this was. Again, at about 5:00 A.M., as the sun was coming up, we noticed the same rustling. It turned out that several thousand bats had taken up residence in the walls of the cabins. They would fly out in the evening and then return in the morning just as the sun was about to come up. Fortunately, they were quiet during the day, as the bats slept during that period. I didn't think it was much of a problem, as the bats weren't bothering us and we weren't bothering them, and the fishing was fairly good. But the ladies saw it differently. They did not appreciate having thousands of bats within a few inches of their heads as they were trying get an extra hour of sleep in the morning.

The final straw occurred on our flight back to San Jose. We were detained by authorities when we landed there. Officials completely ransacked the small airplanes that we were on because someone had tipped them off that we were smuggling drugs. I could envision us locked up in a Costa Rican jail as the perfect ending to the trip. Fortunately, no drugs were found, but it would have been easy for someone to conceal them in small planes flying in and out of the jungle.

So I guess it's no wonder that Nancy is a little suspicious of my fishing expeditions. Even our friends are a little leery when I suggest fishing destinations that look good to me.

Even though Nancy and I have had to find something besides fishing and camping to do together to relax and unwind, she has always understood how important it is for my peace of mind to be outdoors. For me, time spent in the silence and beauty of nature helps me to make sense of the world and sort through the chaos of a fast-paced life. Getting close to God's creation, the more remote the better, puts my life and purpose into perspective.

Early in the morning, just before dawn, everything is so still. As the sun starts to come up, it's almost as though the world is waking. For me, it's often a spiritual experience. Experiencing God's creation—not just the sky and the water and the fish, but other wildlife too, such as geese, ducks and occasional deer (and in Alaska, grizzlies, which I enjoy immensely)—reminds me that

I am a part of it, too. It all fits together. It's so difficult for me to imagine, on mornings like those, that anyone could believe that there's no one behind it all; to me, it is never more undeniable that there is a Creator than when I am fishing.

Fishing is a common biblical theme. You may recall that Jesus' disciples Peter, James, and John were fishermen. After His death, Jesus appeared to the disciples as they were returning from a night of fishing. He had prepared breakfast for them and told them to cast their net on one side of the boat, where they caught a large number of fish. Nancy and I were in Israel two years ago and, remembering this story, I got up before dawn and stood beside the Sea of Galilee as the sun came up over the Golan Heights. Fishing boats, which had been out all night, were coming to shore. I could imagine that the scene was very much like it was 2,000 years ago. It was the most memorable moment of the whole trip, transporting me back in time to the place where Jesus conducted the major part of His ministry.

Back when I was coaching, there would be a few times every season when I wanted to escape from the pressure of the crowds, the games, the press and constant commotion to wet a line. I would think, *If I could just take one day off to go fishing, everything would be okay.* But, of course, I couldn't do it. The football season was what it was—wanting to go fishing and being able to go were two different things. When the season and recruiting were over, though, I'd try to get away for a few days. I vividly remember being determined one Father's Day to celebrate by going fishing. Nancy disagreed, so I was in a full pout. To make amends, Nancy bought me a stuffed fish pillow to salve my hurt feelings. This only made matters worse for me. To this day, that pillow remains a symbol of our differing views on all issues relating to fishing.

Some people lose themselves in a golf game; some people feel best when they run. I feel most alive and renewed when I am fishing (for trout, salmon, walleyes, bass, blue gills and crappies, among others . . . and I particularly enjoy fly-fishing, but any fishing will do!).

Time to Fly

Obviously, my passion for fishing, at times, was a bit disruptive to our family life. I must admit that I had one other interest that was also somewhat problematic. In the early 1980s, I was asked to speak at a Fellowship of Christian Athletes dinner in Wichita, Kansas, and was asked to bring one of my players along who might be willing to share his testimony. We had a linebacker, Steve McWhirter, who was a very committed Christian and a good speaker. So I asked Steve to go with me.

The FCA people in Wichita said they would fly us down and back. Steve and I were out at the airport at the appointed time, waiting for the pilot. As we waited, a corporate jet pilot landed and walked into the flight service. He commented to us that the weather was really bad and was getting worse. We weren't sure anyone would come to pick us up, but not long after, a pilot arrived in a twin-engine push-pull airplane that was rather old. (The "push-pull" means that there was a conventional propeller on the front of the fuselage but also a propeller in the back of the fuselage to "push" the airplane.) With the weather being unsettled and this rather unconventional old airplane being our sole means of transportation, Steve and I were a little apprehensive. We had made a commitment, though, so we got on the plane.

It wasn't too long before the clouds really closed in on us. It began to hail, beating on the airplane so hard that it sounded as though the plane was going to disintegrate. We also were getting tossed around rather badly. I looked at the pilot, who was perspiring heavily, and could tell that he was scared to death. I began to speculate on what might happen if he either passed out or had a heart attack. I knew that Steve and I had our lives in the pilot's hands. We did eventually come through the storm and landed in Wichita but were sufficiently shook up that we rented a car and drove the 300 miles back to Lincoln.

That incident, along with others like it, led me to believe that because I was often flying with people I didn't know, in equipment that was sometimes unreliable, it would be a good idea if I learned how to fly. That way, if something happened to the pilot, I could at least take over the airplane. So I began flying lessons. I soloed in a fairly short time and even went on to get an instrument rating. Finally, when I felt I was ready, I decided to take my family to Colorado on a skiing trip.

We loaded the single engine Piper Saratoga with all of our clothing and gear and, with my wife and three children on board, I started my taxi roll. When I hit 85 knots on the airspeed indicator, I pulled back on the wheel, as this was when I normally would lift off; however, all of my flight training had been with only one passenger—the instructor—and there had been no baggage on board. The plane, being more heavily loaded, did not take off as it had when it I'd had only the instructor on board. Rather, the nose wheel came off the runway about three feet and then settled back down to the runway with a thud, which naturally alarmed my family considerably, even though it was not dangerous.

Since it was obvious that the plane was not going to take off as it had when I had been doing my flight training, I went back to the starting point on the runway, added a notch of flaps and eventually got the airplane airborne, although my family by then was very uneasy. Shortly after takeoff, we noted that the passenger side door was not completely closed. Nancy was certain that the door was going to fly open and we would all be sucked out. This was not the case, but I landed the plane, latched the door and then took off once again.

We made it to the Denver area without further difficulty, but I had elected to fly into Stapleton International Airport rather than one of the small outlying airports in the area. (This was before the new airport in Denver was built, so Stapleton had all of the commercial traffic going in and out of Denver.) As we approached the runway, much to my family's dismay, we had a large commercial airliner about 150 yards off our right wing and another commercial airliner about 150 yards off our left wing. (Of course, these airliners were landing on different runways than we were, but this was not immediately obvious to my family.)

To add to this difficulty, we also were landing with a tremendous crosswind. I had practiced some crosswind landings, but never one with a wind this strong. As a result, the airplane was angled at almost 45 degrees to the runway as we came in. I knew that the landing was not going to be pretty. We hit and lurched a little bit as the plane lined itself out. The landing, along with the proximity of the commercial airliners, had all of my passengers wondering what they had gotten themselves into.

We had a good vacation skiing, but on the way back, we encountered a great deal of turbulence. My son, Mike, became very ill, and everyone else's stomachs were upset as well. My debut as a family pilot was off to a very bad start.

A few weeks later, Nancy, my daughters and I were flying to Ogallala, Nebraska, where we had a cabin. As I was getting closer to Ogallala, I could see a huge cloud bank ahead of us to the west. I soon realized that the cloud bank was going to intercept us before we could get to Ogallala, and it looked like there were going to be some very strong winds, rain and hail in the cloud. So I began to look for an alternate airport.

Gothenburg, Nebraska, was below us. I realized the storm was rapidly moving east, so I descended as fast as I could into the Gothenburg Airport, which has a short cement runway. I came in at a faster-than-normal flying speed in an effort to get on the ground before the storm hit. and I couldn't get the plane to quit flying. Eventually we did touch down, but before I could get the plane stopped, we went off the end of the runway and onto the grass for about 50 yards. We were never in any serious danger but I was not able to convince Nancy and my daughters of that fact.

As a result, much like fishing, I was pretty much consigned to flying by myself from that point on. I flew to speaking engagements and took recruiting trips around the Midwest, but I eventually had to admit to myself that this was a rather dangerous hobby. I would go six months without flying at all during the football season and then once recruiting season came, I would retrain, get my license current and fly for the next few months before the next season began. This type of sporadic flying and retraining was an unhealthy way to approach being a pilot. So after 10 years or so, I gave it up. It wasn't quite the family-friendly activity that I had once hoped it might be.

Surprisingly Strong

Nancy may not be fond of bears or wild about flying in small planes with me, but she is tough in ways that some people might find surprising.

Until we had children, Nancy taught fifth grade and was truly gifted as an educator. When our son, Mike, was born, she became a full-time mom to him and eventually to our daughters, Ann and Suzanne. We were fortunate that this was an option for our family; many families today don't feel as if they have the choice to have one parent stay at home with their children. I can't imagine what we would have done with Nancy continuing to work and me coaching. Nancy truly was the glue that kept our family together and whole.

Sometimes I wonder how critical it is for both parents to work. When I was growing up, we didn't have much money, had only one car, and lived in a very small house in an average neighborhood, yet my mom was at home full time. People at that time didn't think that they needed all of the things that seem to be "necessities" today. Having a mom who is there when you come home from school is more important than a bigger house, three TV sets, three cars and a vacation at Disneyworld. Of course, I understand that in many families a working mom (or dad) is critical to keeping food on the table, and both parents (or a single mom) working is the only option.

The life of a coach's wife is not all a bed of roses. There are stretches of five or six months a year when it's all football all the time, with hardly a moment to spare for anything else. Nancy went to every parent-teacher conference that I could not attend, and every junior-high and high-school game when I was on the road. Our children are the fine people they are today mostly because of her.

Nancy sat in Memorial Stadium for every Huskers game and heard me called every name you could imagine. She supported and encouraged our kids when they were razzed at school after

Nebraska lost a game (sometimes on Monday morning after a loss, they would beg to stay home from school). She never let frustration (and I know there was frustration sometimes) get the best of her—in fact, I often did not know when these things happened because she was determined to take care of whatever problems arose on her own.

There were a few times after we lost a game that were downright nasty, but Nancy toughed it out. We would sit at home on Saturday night after a loss with the phone off the hook because we learned pretty early that once folks had been drinking for a few hours, the phone would start ringing—drunks would call our home from bars to harangue and insult me and the team. There were a few times when Nancy picked up the phone to hear threats delivered in the most vulgar language imaginable. One time, our mailbox was blown up by a cherry bomb, presumably by an angry fan. Most of our fans, however, were very decent.

When I was out of town for away games or for recruiting, Nancy slept on the couch. (I didn't find this out until much later in our marriage.) She was afraid that if someone tried to break in, she wouldn't hear from our bedroom. She slept on the couch to protect our kids from anything that might happen.

I remember reading about Archie Griffin, who was a Heisman Trophy winner from Ohio State University. He talked about how his dad had worked two jobs to support their family when Archie was growing up. Because his dad was gone in the morning before he woke up and got home after he went to bed, Archie hardly ever saw him. But Archie said that he always knew his dad loved him and was doing what needed to be done to provide for his family.

I think my kids know that I care deeply for them, and that my job was the way I provided for our family while they were growing up. Still, there are times that I wonder if my absence was worth it, was it fair? But I'm so thankful that Nancy was there for them each and every day! Any success and happiness our family has experienced has been, I think, due in large part to her.

When I was elected to Congress, Nancy and I were presented with a different challenge in regard to our living arrangement. When you represent a large congressional district like the Third District of Nebraska, which is largely rural, it means that you are going to be traveling from Washington to your home state and then spending quite a bit of time in the District every week. We rented an apartment in Washington, and I left home on Monday or Tuesday morning and returned on Thursday or Friday. Nancy occasionally went to Washington, but she wasn't there more than five or six times a year, and those trips were usually when there was some special occasion in Washington, such as the White House Christmas party or a congressional retreat. This meant that Nancy was home alone at least three nights a week.

The complicating factor was that I was often in the Western part of the state even on the weekends. Nancy accompanied me on some of those trips throughout the Third District as well as most when I campaigned for governor. However, we were apart quite a lot, and at the latter stages of one's life, this is something that one doesn't anticipate. Fortunately, we have children and grandchildren in Nebraska, and Nancy has many friends, so she managed to have a reasonably good life even though I was not around as much as I would have liked.

Members of Congress have a difficult dilemma, in that those with small children have the almost impossible task of figuring out how to manage their lives as representatives as well as parents. I have seen congressmen move their familes to Washington only to find that they are actually back in their districts as much as they are in Washington because of congressional recesses, weekend travel to their districts, and so on. On the other hand, if your family is in your district, you are still in Washington much of every week. It is a very hard way to live, whether you are older like Nancy and I, or are younger with children.

Nancy is my favorite person. If I regret anything about our life together, it's the busyness. When I was coaching, I was basically "missing in action" for five or six months a year, and Nancy was extraordinarily patient with that situation. She did a lot of the day-to-day parenting and nurturing of our children, and I tried to make up the lost time during the off-season. I'm incredibly thankful that, even given the demanding nature of my coaching career, I have strong and loving relationships with Nancy, our children and our grandchildren.

All in all, Nancy has been the best partner I could have wished for. She has rolled with the punches with uncommon grace and good spirits. I cannot imagine my life without her.

Coaching and Fathering

My son, Mike, was the starting quarterback for my alma mater, Hastings College, for three years, and I missed most of his games. His games were usually on Saturday afternoons and Nebraska's games were usually on Saturday afternoons—and being two places at one time is a mighty hard thing to accomplish. If Hastings played at a different time than the Cornhuskers, however, I was there. I got films of those games I couldn't attend and studied them as thoroughly as my own team's films.

All three of my children played sports of one kind or another. Mike played football and basketball. Ann played basketball.

Suzanne played volleyball and tennis. And I'll tell you this: I wish I'd seen more of their games. It was very hard, sometimes, to be a coach *and* be a father.

His senior year of high school, Mike started the season as quarterback. The first three games of the season, his team played three of the top-rated schools in the state—and lost all three by one or two points. After that third game, Mike's coach decided to replace him with an up-and-coming junior, and Mike sat out the rest of the season.

As a coach, I could understand that coach's decision (I might not have made the same call, but I could understand his reasoning). But as a father, it was very painful to watch. I suddenly felt very empathetic to the parents who had called me over the years, distraught about their son's lack of playing time or whatever—their hurt or anguish was very real, and important to respect. And that experience brought home to me in a new way the impact that coaches' decisions have on their players, for good and for ill. (Fortunately, basketball season was right around the corner and Mike didn't have to sit on the bench for long. But watching him go through that senior football season was difficult.)

I think all three of my kids probably experienced a different kind of pressure in the realm of athletics than many other kids. For whatever reason, there is an expectation that a coach's child will excel in that area of life. I tried very hard not to add to that pressure and to encourage my children to try many different things to discover what they liked and were good at. At the same time, I felt (and still strongly feel) that competitive sports are an important aspect of physical, mental and character development. I wanted my children to have those experiences and opportunities.

I'm not sure that I always got the balance right between letting them explore and choose for themselves and encouraging them to excel and stick to it. There was a period of time when some of Mike's friends took up other interests (such as skateboarding) and quit playing sports. He wanted to go with them at times, but I encouraged him to continue playing. He wasn't happy at the time, but I'm pretty sure he was appreciative as time went on. It's a very hard call for a parent to make, because the "sweet spot" is somewhere between letting kids do whatever they want at a time when they're not fully equipped to make informed choices and pushing them against their will to do something for which they have no desire or aptitude. I do know for certain, from watching other parents live their own dreams out through the lives of their children, that pushing kids too hard into activities for which they have no interest or aptitude can be very destructive.

Coaching is very interesting and rewarding, in that you become something of a surrogate parent to a great many young people. By my count, I coached somewhere in the neighborhood of 2,000 young men during my coaching career, and I can remember most of them fairly well. Their joys became my joys, their hurts became my hurts, and I wanted the very best for them, not only in athletics but also in their academic careers and in their lives after they left school. It has been very rewarding to interact with these former players on a regular basis and to see them grow and mature into responsible adults and parents themselves.

The thing I had to continually guard against was being like a parent to all of those football players while not being an adequate parent to my own children. I was reminded continuously of how important parenting is as I saw the dysfunction and the pain in the lives of many of my players. Some of them were fatherless and it was easy to discern that fatherlessness had created some real emotional gaps in their lives, which made their lives very difficult. With Nancy's help, however, I believe that I was able to be a reasonably good father in spite of the time crunch that I was under so much of the time.

Losing Is Never Fun

Obviously, football was a big part of our family's life. Nancy and I took our children with us when Nebraska played in bowl games, so our kids were afforded the chance to travel to parts of the country that they otherwise might not have visited. But sometimes the intensity of our family's involvement in Nebraska's wins and losses caused unexpected and even humorous family tension.

The Oklahoma-Nebraska rivalry is well-known in the world of college football as one of the greatest football series of all time. Until the Big XII Conference was formed, Nebraskans across the state (and presumably Oklahomans, too) turned on their TVs after Thanksgiving dinner to battle out their storied rivalry (and many in both states are still upset that current conference rules deny the two schools their annual match-up).

One year when my daughter Ann was five or six years old, we lost to Oklahoma for the third year in a row. When I got home from the game, tired and feeling down about the loss, Ann announced that she was moving to Oklahoma—she was sick of losing, and if we couldn't figure out how to win, she wanted to live where they knew how. A loss to Oklahoma was a major disaster to most Nebraskans and my kids knew that they would get an earful at school on Monday, so Ann decided that if we couldn't beat them, she was going to join them.

Obviously, Ann felt the sting of those losses to Oklahoma, but all of my children were aware of what was at stake with every game. My son, Mike, recently sent an email to his customers reflecting on his memories of the 1984 Orange Bowl game with Miami, which was for the national championship. His memory of this game, when he held my phone line cords on the sideline, demonstrates the feelings of family members as they watch things unravel in a big game. The story is as follows:

This was it. I couldn't believe it, but it had come down to this. NU needed 9 yards on 4th down to keep the drive and our hopes for the 1983 national title alive. I had thought it would be a cakewalk, a coronation, against an overmatched unknown Miami University squad on this sultry evening in Miami. Bernie Kosar had other ideas, as did his showman coach Howard Schnellenberger.

The game had been a surreal progression of uphill struggles. Unbelievable yardage and points given up to a guy who looked like he would trip over a crack in the sidewalk because of his awkward saunter and goofy big feet. Turner Gill, one of the great gamers of all time, had single handedly kept us in the game by the skin of our teeth, twice engineering 14 point comebacks during a game that seemed like it was being played at double speed. When Miami jumped ahead in the first half we thought it was a fluke, and that we would run on by them like we had all year—there was plenty of time. And then, in the snap of a finger, it was half way through the 4th quarter and they had another 14-point lead!

There was a quiet stillness in the small space surrounding coach and Turner, and even though I was less than two feet away, I couldn't hear a thing they were saying to each other. Both of their faces were focused, relaxed from having been in the "battle," yet with an intense understanding in their eyes of the magnitude of the situation.

Turner turned and jogged back to the huddle at Miami's 35-yard line. The jet roar of the crowd cranked up steadily from the time he departed the sideline to the time he had the offense set over the ball. I wiped my hand through my hair, my dad's headphone cords tightly gripped in my right hand—too nervous to breathe. How had it come down to this? Did Turner have one more super-human feat left in his bag of unending tricks? Even as a college quarterback myself, I couldn't fathom the pressure. I knew it would come down to him on this play.

He bobbed his head to the left and right as he barked out the false audible and snap count—only 20 yards away from me, yet all I could hear was the deafening white noise of the crazed stands. Like a silent movie, he gave the final count and ball cracked into his hands from center and he turned around to his right sharply to face the defensive end, I couldn't believe it! My dad had called an option on 4th and 9+. In that split second I felt sorry for Turner—it was too much to ask. But Turner then looked up at the corner back or monster back, I couldn't tell, he now had the ball up under his shoulder as he stutter-stepped down the line—now I really couldn't believe it!

After all this poor guy had been through on this night, carrying the whole team almost by himself—running options, dancing through the defense like Walter Payton at his finest, twisting and turning his slender body to avoid the big hits and gain the extra yard, and dropping back time and time again zipping the ball on a rope to targets scampering down field—now he was being asked to execute the most difficult play in the book, a run pass option! No more than a nano second after peeking toward the slanting receiver did Turner pull the ball down and proceed hard toward the end of Miami's line. He took two more full strides and then perfectly flipped the ball to a rounding Jeff Smith, just as Turner was taking the hit from the optioned end.

Turner's part in the play was done, and to my relief for him, he once again had executed perfectly, and under the most difficult circumstances anyone could imagine. The play was now on the far sideline and it was a blur of spraying sand and dirt as spikes tore the turf in an upfield sprint. Smith had turned upfield! White shirts were on the ground! It looked like the first down was in hand! The fever pitch of the crowd was lost as my own euphoria and the Nebraska sideline began to poise for an explosive celebration.

Smith was dancing down the sideline and the Hurricanes were stumbling and grabbing at air! He bolted at the 10 and took two huge steps and lunged into the end zone! No one could believe it as we jumped and high fived and shouted back at the crowd who now stood in shocked disbelief.

As I took in the scene and felt the rush of blood to my limbs and a relaxing sense that the nightmare was about to end, I suddenly felt a jolt in my hands. I looked to the right and saw my dad give me a quick stern look as his head had been pulled back by his headphones when I had failed to give him enough slack. He had bolted up field to send in the two-point play almost at the moment Smith crossed the goal line. He came to Irving Fryar to tell him the play, while Turner came toward to the sideline, fully aware that he was going to turn around and go back out to get the two points. My dad only paused for a second to consider the possible plays. Once again it was like watching a silent film as the buzz of anticipation from the crowd and the barking of the players drowned out the quiet plans being spelled out that would determine the fate of one of the greatest teams in college football history. Despite what was now at stake, there was only so much energy these guys could have. Most of us would have been on intravenous fluid at half time.

30-31. Forty-eight seconds left on the game clock. No overtime. No thought, maybe not even the knowledge, that a tie would clinch the national title. Not by the guys in that huddle of huddles, not by me, not by anyone wearing red until more than 24 hours later. It was win or lose, national title or nothing. One play, one moment in time, to represent forever the years of toil by the seniors, and decades by the coaches. Very similar to an Olympic final, only there weren't any silver or bronze medals to be had.

Fryar gave Turner the play and they turned back to the huddle, this time 30 yards downfield to where the ball rested at the 3-yard line. The noise only half-heartedly started up this time. The crowd, too, had realized NU's nightmare was over, and Miami's dream may have only been just that—a dream. But they knew they had a role to play and maybe still a slight chance of stopping this wizard in red, Turner Gill.

As we broke the huddle, they got their throats back into it and made a great effort to come to full pitch. With his team set over the ball, Turner looked over the defense before he lowered his right shoulder and bounced down into his crouch under center. His head turning and left and right, he called out his signals and faced forward and nodded sharply on the snap count. The ball flashed into his hands and again he turned right, and again the ball came up under his shoulder as he peered over the end and into Miami's backfield toward the right end zone. He stutter stepped twice and this time, he unleashed the ball forward.

My hopes for my dad and for Turner and this team fluttered through the air toward the target. It had been a long 11 years watching my dad as head coach. Seeing the endless hours, the non-stop grind, the heartbreaks, the highs and lows, was all about to have been worth it. This was going to be the greatest team to have played the college game. The "scoring explosion" was going to have saved the day. The "can't win the big one" label was going to fade into history.

The ball hung for a second. I saw Jeff Smith turn over his shoulder in the flat and put out his hands—the ball was on plane and . . . tipped, bounce, glance off the shoulder and flip to the ground. There was a moment in the stadium where everyone processed who was going to get to celebrate. Then the floodgates opened, and the madness ensued worse than ever. The crazies in the stands danced and shouted and threw things into the air. The raucous music blared out of the Orange Bowl speakers "Hurricane Warning" over and over. The opposite sideline, which seemed a mile away, jumped and leaped and zig-zagged like popping corn. Hugs and slaps and jubilation all the way around.

Schnellenberger's coronation as King of Miami was the only coronation taking place tonight. The consummate "David," Bernie Kosar, flashed the broadest, whitest smile that any 19-year-old kid ever smiled as he strode along the sideline waiting to go back in to take a final snap or two.

My dad looked out over the field with a distant stare, perhaps thinking about all the blood, sweat and tears that went into this, and could he do it again? Would he ever get such a talented group together again, one that could hog-tie OU's athletes and confound Barry Switzer? Did he have the energy—was it worth it? I don't know if those were his thoughts. But they were mine. And I hurt for my dad. No one worked harder, and no one did it more the right way, and no one deserved it more. It wasn't fair. These guys across the field had backed into this. It was a fluke. It was pomp over circumstance and they had managed to pull it off. If only we could get this bunch to play in Lincoln, what a massacre that would be.

The final gun fired and the party continued as portions of the stands flooded onto the field, wildly congratulating the guys in white. Miami was never happier. Schnellenberger was lifted onto waiting shoulders and paraded around the field. My dad forced his way to midfield and found Howard to shake his hand. And then he turned to run through the throng and into the despondent tiny locker room, probably trying to think of what to say to the team. Turner remained kneeling on the sideline with hand on helmet, starting into the mad scene before him, and then rose to congratulate a few white shirts. I slapped him on the shoulder, hoping he could somehow know that he was forever a champion with the heart of a lion for the way he had played.

I went and sat in the car waiting just outside the gate. The City of Miami officer who was my dad's driver was a true Husker fan, and he was silent with a drawn tired look. I sat in the silence waiting for my dad. My ears buzzed a little from the 4-hour rock concert they had just been subjected to. My nerves were shut down. I had that deep ache that comes when there is nothing you can do about something so painful to someone you love. Charlie McBride got in the car, and he too sat silently for a bit, rubbing his head and muttering a thing or two. My dad came and got in the passenger seat, with the same distant look he had at the end of the game.

The next morning he went recruiting, back in the saddle.

It wasn't for another 10 years, with another wizard in red as QB, that we got back to being one play away. Unfinished Business finally and forever was taken care of one year later, and this time—that wild orange and white hoard fell silent in the fourth quarter, and never made another peep. A fitting end to that grand old Orange Bowl.

Obviously, Mike, as my son, probably saw my actions through rose-colored glasses, but I believe his words show how the children of coaches feel the slings and arrows of fate very strongly as they watch their dad coach and sometimes come up short. Mike also wrote with the perspective of one who was a quarterback, so he empathized strongly with Turner Gill and appreciated all Turner brought to the game. We were short of a national championship by one play on several occasions. I always hurt for the players who gave great effort yet never experienced winning a championship. None of them deserved it more than Turner.

Saying Yes to My Family

Before I decided to run for Congress, a coaching job at Michigan State University opened up. I got a call from the school's president, who was hoping to hire me. He was offering a lot of money. It was tempting. Even though I had been out of coaching for only a few months, I missed it badly. I didn't think I could sit in the stands, watch Nebraska play, and have no involvement in what was happening on the field.

Nancy and I considered the offer, talking through pros and cons. One evening in the midst of our decision-making, the phone rang. It was my grandson, Will, who was five years old at the time. He was crying and could barely get a word out. When Will finally caught his breath enough to tell me what was the matter, he said that he didn't want us to move to Michigan.

That did it for me. There was no way we could leave our children and grandchildren—even for an attractive coaching job.

Likewise, as I mentioned in a previous chapter, when Karl Rove called from the White House to ask if I would think about being considered to fill the post of Secretary of Agriculture, I eventually had to turn him down. To say yes to my family, I had to say no to a possible opportunity that many politicians could not refuse.

When I retired from coaching in 1997, the University of Nebraska did me the great honor of naming the football field after me. Thousands of Cornhusker fans were in the stadium that day to show their support, but it was my family's support and love through the years that meant the most to me. As they uncovered the portion of the field painted with the words "Tom Osborne Field," it was never more obvious to me that Nancy and our children deserved the lion's share of the audience's applause. Championship wins are a wonderful thing, but relationships and family are what life is all about.

SERVING

For when the one Great Scorer comes to write against your name, it matters not that you won or lost, but how you played the game.

GRANTLAND RICE

Players Who Served

I have emphasized the importance of a servant mentality and how it can play a significant role in every aspect of life. I have had the honor of working with many people who have exemplified what it means to consider others first. Perhaps none have done it better than Brook Berringer. Brook was a quarterback for the University of Nebraska in the mid-1990s. Brook hailed from Goodland, Kansas, a small town in the western part of the state, and before he came to Nebraska, I doubt that he had played in front of a crowd of more than 500 people.

Tommie Frazier, a quarterback from Bradenton, Florida, came to school about the same time. He had played in the Florida state championship game in front of more than 60,000 people. He was all-star material from the get-go, and he started for us as a freshman. He led the team to victory in the first four games of the '94 season, and then was diagnosed with blood clots in his leg. The situation was very serious and the doctors told us that he would probably not play the remainder of the season—and might never play again.

We needed a quarterback to fill the gap, and we turned to Brook. Honestly, we didn't know exactly what to expect—Tommie had been our go-to guy and much of our offense was structured around his playing. On top of that, the players were concerned about Tommie and uncertain about how to move forward without his leadership. We needn't have worried. Brook stepped in and led the team to eight straight wins, and gave the players the confidence they needed to pull together.

Brook did all this with a lung that collapsed twice. The doctors reinflated it and told us that if it happened again, Brook was finished for the season. (Thankfully, it did not happen again.) Actually, Brook's condition was serious enough that we started our number three quarterback, Matt Turman, against Kansas State in Manhattan, Kansas. Matt performed well, but the game was tight and Brook wanted to play. I asked the doctor if it was possible to play Brook after having had his lung collapsed on two previous Saturdays. The doctor said it would be okay if he played as long as he "didn't get hit." Naturally, a player not getting hit in football is hard to guarantee; however, Brook did enter the game in the second half and did a great job of leading us to victory.

The pivotal game during the season was against Colorado in Lincoln. Colorado had great players and was ranked number two in the nation. We were ranked either two or three at the time, depending on the poll, and we played a nearly flawless football game. We won the game 24-7. Our defense was outstanding, and Brook played a great game. That game against Colorado is often overlooked when people think about some of the most meaningful games that the University of Nebraska has played over the years; however, it is one that I will never forget. I thought that we played so well that we showed we were quite possibly going to be the top team in the country that year. We continued to win and finished the regular season with a 13-3 win over the University of Oklahoma in Norman.

By the time the bowl game in Miami rolled around, Tommie Frazier had recovered to the point that he was allowed to play. We had a major scrimmage prior to the bowl game and Tommie graded slightly better than Brook, so Tommie started—but Brook came in and threw a touchdown pass during the second quarter. They both played significant roles in the game, and we won 24-17. Beating Miami on their own field was very difficult to do, as Miami had lost only 1 home game in more than 70 games in the

Orange Bowl Stadium. Any team that played Miami in the Orange Bowl was at a considerable disadvantage, because they were playing on their home field in front of their home crowd, usually in high humidity.

Here's where the servant part comes in: At the start of the 1995 season, Nebraska had two great quarterbacks who together had led our team to a national championship the previous year. Who would be the starter and who the backup? We decided that we would grade every snap during our fall camp going into the 1995 season. This included scrimmages and practices. At the end of fall camp, the grades were almost identical; however, Brook Berringer had one interception in our final scrimmage and Tommie had none. So we named Tommie Frazier as our starting quarterback and Brook was once again the backup.

Now, it wouldn't be too hard to find a quarterback of Brook Berringer's caliber who, put in a similar position, would have caused dissention. There were many team members who would have supported him had Brook decided to do so—he had won the players' gratitude and loyalty when he had led them through such a trying time of uncertainty the previous year. And many players would have supported Tommie. Yet Brook chose to sacrifice what some might have seen as his right to raise a fuss in favor of supporting Tommie and the team. He was always encouraging, always positive. The times he did get to play during that 1995 season, he played very well. Tommie had a great 1995 season and finished second in the Heisman Trophy balloting. Had the final vote been held after the Fiesta Bowl win against Florida, in which Tommie played a fantastic game, I'm sure that he would have won the Heisman.

In a 2006 readers' poll on ESPN.com, the 1995 Cornhuskers were voted the best college football team of all time.[1] There is no doubt in my mind that the chemistry, heart and cohesiveness of that team is due in no small part to the servanthood of Brook Berringer. Without his self-sacrifice, the team might easily have disintegrated into factions instead of coming together as the best team that I ever had the privilege of coaching.

Brook was a man of uncommonly strong faith. He was an excellent role model and did a great deal of community outreach, speaking to school children, visiting hospitals and reading to kids. He influenced many of Nebraska's players to seek deeper meaning in their lives and I'm confident that, if he had lived, he would have made a similar impact on players in the NFL. He was widely expected to be selected in the 1996 draft and many anticipated watching him come fully into his own as a player in professional football, but tragedy struck. Brook, an amateur airplane pilot, was flying a small plane when it crashed near Raymond, Nebraska, two days before the NFL draft. He was killed in the crash, along with his friend Tobey Lake, who was also his fiancée's brother.

Even through his death, Brook's life impacted people. So often when we're young, we believe that we're invincible, that nothing can touch us. It's a sad reality, but often it's only when a young person's life is cut short that other young people are challenged to evaluate what they want their lives to be about. Nearly 50,000 people honored Brook in a ceremony held in Memorial Stadium prior to the 1996 spring football game. That crowd stood as a witness to the great person, football player and servant that Brook was.

Country music group Sawyer Brown wrote and performed "The Nebraska Song" in Brook's memory at the Nebraska State Fair the following year. The lyrics eloquently capture the servant mentality that was a hallmark of Brook's entire life: "I'll work hard and I'll do my part, you won't hear me complain; I'll never go down easy, I swear I'll pull my weight."[2]

When I think about athletes who had a servant mentality, another player comes to mind very quickly, and that is Roger Craig. In 1982, we had a very fine football team with two great running backs. Roger Craig was going into his senior year, and Mike Rozier had transferred in from Coffeyville Junior College. They were the best pair of backs I ever coached. The problem was that they both played the same position—I-back—and we felt we needed to get both of them on the field at one time as much as possible.

We talked to Roger about the possibility of moving to fullback. At fullback, he would not carry the ball as much and would have to do more blocking. Roger was as good as any I-back in the country and could have easily rushed for 1,500 to 2,000 yards during that 1982 season, but he was willing to accept the challenge of moving to fullback to become more of a blocker. Roger still carried the ball a fair amount, but not anywhere near as much as he would have at I-back. He was pretty much limited to the inside running game that a fullback normally does, as opposed to running both outside and inside as an I-back would do.

Roger could have refused the switch, complained or pouted, but he never said a word. He just went to work. We had a great team in 1982, with a close loss at Penn State early in the year that could have gone either way. Had we won that game, we would have been national champions that year. (Actually, strangely enough, Penn State also had a loss that year—a fairly bad one to Alabama—but they were named national champions and we weren't.)

Mike Rozier went on to win the Heisman Trophy after the next season, 1983, based on the statistics and the platform he had earned during the 1982 season. A major part of Mike's success had to do with Roger Craig's willingness to make the switch to fullback.

It wasn't all negative for Roger, however. The San Francisco 49ers saw something in him that they really liked. They saw a great runner, a good blocker, and an unselfish player. They took Roger fairly high in the draft and he teamed up with Tom Rathman, another one of our backs, to be a key element in several Super Bowl championship teams at San Francisco.

Fortunately, we had a number of players who were like Brook Berringer and Roger Craig: players who sacrificed individual playing time, statistics and recognition to make the team better. They brought out the best in everyone around them and were always the kind of players I looked for.

Servant-Coach

As I wrote early in this book, each of us is called on to play various roles throughout our lives. It is my belief that in every phase of life and in every professional and relational role we play, we should choose servanthood over selfishness. Of course this is very idealistic thinking, as we live in a very "me first" society and servanthood is often the last thing people think about. As I reflect back over my life, I can see many times when I have been selfish and have not been a servant; however, I have intended to serve in the roles I have held for the last 40-plus years.

When I first started coaching, there were no such things as "shoe contracts," a phrase that is as common now in college sports as "sponsored by Gatorade®." When Nebraska was first approached by one of the leading shoe manufacturers about setting up a sponsorship for which they would furnish shoes to all of our players, one of the offers on the table made me very uncomfortable: The company would pay me if the athletes wore that company's brand of shoe.

Well, that just didn't seem right to me—and I wasn't the only coach who thought so. Why should coaches get paid for what our players wear on their feet? Several head coaches, all around the same time, decided that such a thing was not in the best interests of our players. Bo Schembechler at Michigan refused to take the "shoe money" (as it came to be called), and at Nebraska we used the money to set up a post-graduate scholarship fund for players who decided to pursue further education.

There is a stark contrast between coaches who are in it for themselves and those who serve their players. On the one hand, you see coaches like the young high school coach I met on a recruiting trip years ago. "Man, I just love this job," he told me. "It's just amazing the power that I have over these kids. I can tell 'em to do almost anything and they'll do it." I was appalled. All I could think was, *I'm glad my son is not playing for this guy.*

Coaching, for that young man, was about gratifying his ego by exercising power. For others, it is about financial gain or publicity or status. Yet many other people who choose to play the role of coach do so out of a sincere love for players and their sport. They put their players first, never putting someone in the game who is at serious risk for injury or benching a player out of spite. They refuse to cut corners when it comes to recruiting or to bend or break the rules to get an edge over the competition. They honor and respect their opponents in word and in deed, on and off the field.

It's often easy to tell the difference between these two kinds of coaches by looking at their teams. Players coached by self-seeking leaders are often unhappy, even when their team is winning. They often tear others down and lash out when they are threatened, and they have behavior problems that are difficult to get under control.

If a coach has enticed a player using unethical recruiting promises, their relationship is out of balance from the word "go"; a coach who had offered a player illegal inducements once confided to me, "You know, once you've done that, your coach-player relationship is forever altered. He has power over you that he should not have because he can turn you in or use it against you. The whole dynamic is undermined, and in the long run, the team is put at risk."

By contrast, players coached by leaders who put their players' interests ahead of their own usually play with heart, drive and determination even when they are having a tough season; they play hard because they know that their coach will never deliberately sacrifice their welfare for his own. They speak to and act toward their teammates and opponents alike with respect, and they understand that their behavior choices will have an affect on everyone. In short, these players learn under the tutelage of a servant-coach and through the ups and downs of the game, what it means to be a healthy and productive person.

Doug McIntosh, who played UCLA men's basketball under Coach John Wooden, wrote the following about his experience in Wooden's program:

> *In the 39 years since I graduated from UCLA . . . I have told people quite often that every UCLA basketball player who spent time under Coach Wooden's tutelage received more than improved skills. He received a way of thinking about problem-solving and overcoming obstacles. If you paid attention and believed in what*

he said, you not only became a better basketball player, you became a more competent person. He was as much a philosopher as a coach, and he was equally proficient at both activities. My basketball skills I lost long ago, but the life principles he left with me are more valuable today than they were when I first heard them.[3]

This is the kind of impact that a servant-coach can have on a player's life—an impact that will long outlive that player's career on the playing field.

Serving in Political Office

When we opened my congressional office, our policy was to answer each and every piece of constituent mail that we received within 14 days. On an average day, we received between 150 and 200 letters, in addition to the 50 or so emails delivered to the inbox. Answering each one in a timely fashion was a time-consuming and never-ending job, but our view was that responding to our constituents' needs and concerns was the whole point of being a congressional representative.

Serving Nebraska's Third District entailed much more than answering mail, however, and it involved more than giving an occasional speech and marching in parades. I believed that the best way I could serve the residents of the Third District was to listen to their concerns, ideas and aspirations and then articulate a vision for our future. To be an effective leader, one has to be able to paint a picture of what can be and take concrete steps to make the possible happen.

As discussed earlier, one concern I heard again and again from constituents was about the loss of young people from our rural district—young adults were heading off to college and not coming back. An entire way of life was beginning to die out as the older generation retired or passed away and no one came to take their places. How could we stem the tide of "brain drain" and keep Nebraska's best and brightest rooted and growing in our communities?

We thought that one way might be to educate the younger generation on entrepreneurship. If they had the tools to start successful businesses locally, why would they want to let their ideas get lost in the shuffle of Chicago or New York? We put together an entrepreneurial handbook that showed young people the nuts and bolts of starting a business. What's your idea? What's your vision for implementing it? How can you raise capital or get a small business loan? How do you let people know about your product or service? How can you write a grant application? How do you write a business plan? Our vision was to inspire creative and innovative young people to start businesses that would eventually create jobs and prosperity in communities that might have died without them.

A number of communities incorporated entrepreneurial training in their school systems and many used the entrepreneurial handbook as a starting point. I remember visiting Ord, Nebraska, a small town in the central part of the state that had a particularly good entrepreneurial training program. They had young high-school students start businesses from scratch. Students formulated an idea for a business, wrote a business plan, raised enough capital to make a product (this was usually not more than $50 to $100), and then marketed the product.

When I visited the school, several of the students showed me what they were doing as part of their entrepreneurial project. The value of this program was that a student learned what it took to start a business that would have a chance of being successful. In the future, they would not shy away from developing a new business that might employ other people in their community if they ran across an idea that could be financially feasible and productive. Many times, people won't try to start a business because they have no idea how to do it. I know that many small businesses were started throughout the Third District as a result of these entrepreneurial training programs.

I remember a particular young man who lived in Sutton, Nebraska, who hit upon the idea of selling pickled asparagus. This may not sound all that appealing, but he started a business and increased his market share exponentially over a short period of time. He sold thousands of jars of pickled asparagus, which enabled him to finance his way through college. It's my guess that the young man is doing quite well as an entrepreneur today, probably in a small town in Nebraska.

As mentioned earlier, I heard many Third-District residents express their dismay at the growing methamphetamine problem in our state. As in many other parts of the country, meth use was beginning to become an epidemic. Somewhere in the neighborhood of 50 percent of children in Nebraska's foster-care system were there because their parents were meth addicts—these folks had lost their ability to care about anything but the drug, and that included their kids.

There are tremendous social costs to this kind of family breakdown, but there are also financial costs: a dependent meth user costs the U.S. nearly $75,000 per year. Taken together, the annual cost of meth to our society is estimated to be more than $23 billion![4] By my estimate, Nebraska's share of this cost is $1.5 billion annually. That only represents the financial cost—the human cost is even greater. One of my college classmates lost his bright, college student daughter when she got confused in a snow storm, couldn't think or communicate effectively and died from exposure because of meth.

How could our congressional office help to tackle this rampant problem? We decided that one way was to pull together an educational DVD to be shown in Nebraska schools that would inform students about the dangers of methamphetamine and alcohol abuse. Our goal was to get the DVD into the hands of every school administrator in the state within one year and to appear at a school assembly in every high school and middle school in the Third District. John Hanson, my district director, and I spoke at the majority of these convocations. I am certain that many lives were saved in the process. At nearly every presentation, we had students approach us with stories about what meth and alcohol had done to their families. The students were horrified at pictures of what methamphetamine use does to the human body in a relatively short time.

We also tried to work with rural communities on developing alternative ways of doing business. For instance, the southwestern part of the Third District, at that time, was experiencing a progressive cutback on the amount of irrigation water they could use. The hard truth is that there is only so much water to go around, and the cutback was a practical response to that shortage. But what were our constituents to do, and how could we help?

We explored with them the possibility of cultivating alternative crops that required less water to grow. Some residents took this route. We talked with others about creating a pheasant habitat that would attract bird hunters from out of town—this would be an additional income stream for farmers. Some residents found this option to be a good one for them.

Whether our office was tackling meth use, water shortages, brain drain or our bottomless pile of mail, the driving force behind our efforts was to serve the people I was elected to represent. As a matter of fact, we wrote a formal mission statement that stated our purpose was "to serve the people of the Third District of Nebraska." I know that many other politicians view their positions in this way, and I believe these folks are the most effective at their jobs. Our representative democracy *can* be of the people, by the people and for the people, when the goal is to serve rather than be served. Unfortunately, for many in politics, the mission is to get elected or re-elected rather than serve.

One of the best examples of a servant leader that I saw in Congress was a congressman from North Carolina named Robin Hayes. Robin's family had been in the textile business for many years, and many of Robin's constituents were textile workers. These jobs were leaving North Carolina and going overseas, where labor costs are much cheaper.

One night, we had a long session followed by a vote on the Central America Free Trade Agreement (CAFTA). Robin knew that a vote for that trade agreement would be very unpopular in his district, as many people would perceive it as legislation that would cause more jobs to go overseas. Many labor groups were and are opposed to trade agreements, as they would rather see an isolationist approach in which the U.S. erects trade barriers and keeps foreign products out of the United States. The problem with this is that other countries will not buy goods from us in return in a global economy where goods and commodities are sold and traded worldwide. An protectionist approach is therefore self-defeating.

Robin knew very well that his vote for CAFTA could cost him his next election, yet he also believed strongly that CAFTA would serve the greater good in the United States and throughout the world by creating more jobs and trade. The leadership was counting on Robin to help pass the bill, and he eventually pushed the green button in favor of the bill. He had tears in his eyes when he did so, because he knew that his political future was very bleak at that point. Robin had also had voted for Trade Promotion Authority (TPA), which gave the President the ability to move more quickly on trade agreements.

Robin's political opponents pointed out repeatedly that he had cast the "deciding vote" for both CAFTA and TPA. Robin did survive one more election—barely—and then lost in the 2008 elections. However, Robin voted as he did based on principle and what he thought was best for the country rather than getting himself re-elected. I'm not sure how many people in Washington would do what Robin did. There are a few, undoubtedly, but not very many.

Servant-Leader

I have already written at length about the relationship between servanthood and effective leadership, but I'd like to add here two additional thoughts.

The first is to point out what I think is the obvious connection between servanthood and character. Essentially, being a servant demands that one be a person of good character, and vice versa. Honesty, integrity, generosity, a sense of fair play—these are all attributes that we associate with people of good character, and they are remarkably consistent across eras and cultures, as Stephen Covey and others have noted. If anyone wants to be a good leader—that is, if he or she hopes that others will follow him or her—these are essential attributes that must be developed. People may follow a corrupt, charismatic personality or a visionary without substance for a while, but if their leader lacks character, eventually they will find someone else to follow. (There are times, however, as in the case of Adolf Hitler, when it takes a distressingly long time to see what the leader is all about.)

The second point is that a core aspect of being a leader is challenging those who follow us to display good character. Sometimes this aspect of leadership means a willingness to confront followers for bad choices and behaviors. While confrontation makes many people uncomfortable, it is occasionally necessary.

I recruited a young man years ago who was rumored to be a marijuana user in high school. We wanted to offer him a scholarship, but we had a strict no-drugs policy. I decided that the best course of action was to ask him up-front: "We want to recruit players, not problems. Have you used or do you use marijuana?"

The young man said, "No, absolutely not. I would never use drugs." I took him at his word and we moved forward in the process, offering him a scholarship for the following fall.

About three months before players were to report for practice, we sent out a notice that they each had to undergo a physical exam to ensure that they were in good health. We also notified them that they would be drug tested. The players arrived in early August, were given physical exams and were tested for steroids and street drugs. When the young man's results came in, I saw that he had tested positive for marijuana use.

So, I called him in. "Remember what you told me? You said that you had never used marijuana and never would. You weren't honest with me, and by telling a lie, you have broken trust with me. Here's the thing: I still care about you and want to help make you the best player you can be. But from here on out, it's going to be tough. We're going to notify your parents. We're going to send you for a drug evaluation to determine if you need counseling or a drug rehabilitation hospital. We're going to test you weekly from now on. Can you live with that?"

Well, he wasn't happy about it, but he agreed to my terms and joined the team under the conditions that we had set for him. Unfortunately, over the next six months, he tested positive for drug use two more times. According to our policy, he was dismissed for good.

That young man was a fine football player, and I would have liked to have had him on the team. His suspension was not just a loss for him but also a loss for all of us. However, leading in that situation meant challenging that young man to be a better person—in essence, serving his long-term good by sacrificing the team's short-term gain.

About 10 years later, I got a call from the young player. He apologized to me for lying and for his drug use, expressing remorse for his behavior. He was now drug-free after having had a spiritual conversion, and was trying to make things right.

Even though it might entail a short-term loss for the whole group, leaders rarely go wrong when they are determined to serve the character development of their individual followers. Sometimes this service, in the form of a challenge, is rejected at the time only to bear fruit much later. But it is always worth waiting for.

Servant-Mentor

I'll be honest: I am often busy. Being the athletic director at the University of Nebraska means that I go to a lot of meetings. If I'm not in a meeting, I'm on my way to a meeting or on a conference call instead of a meeting.

As busy as this job keeps me, however, there is one appointment that I keep each and every week: The hour that I spend with the young man to whom I am a mentor. My assistant schedules a noon hour once a week when I bring my lunch and eat with him. We talk about school or football (he plays in the youth league) or sometimes fishing. Occasionally, if he's having trouble with his homework, I help him out or talk with his teachers about how he is doing. We try to focus on those things he does well—his strengths.

My time with him is something I never miss because showing up, each and every time, is the most fundamental aspect of being a mentor. When I recruit new mentors for TeamMates, this is the message I try to communicate: Unless you come to mentoring with the mindset of a servant—a deliberate determination to put your mentee's needs ahead of your own for at least an hour a week—you won't be very good at it. Mentoring *is* serving.

There is another young man whose life I've been involved in recently who lost his dad, who played football for Nebraska. His father's death had taken a terrible toll on this young man, and his schoolwork was beginning to suffer. He had been in and out of foster homes and his teachers were concerned about him. The young man's mentor was able to understand that much of what he needed—rather than tutoring or intensive help with his education—was help in processing his grief. We dug up film of his dad playing at Nebraska and gave it to him on DVD, reminding him that if he wanted to follow in his father's footsteps to college, he'd have to knuckle down in his studies. He was proud and pleased as he watched films of his father's football career. His teacher asked him to show the DVD to his class, which he did with great pride. Before long, his grades began to improve. The connection with his father, in the form of that DVD, helped the young man get things back on track. His mentor has been the one constant anchor in his life.

Effective mentoring doesn't happen by accident; it takes a sustained, concerted effort to form a relationship characterized by unconditional love and acceptance.

Fishing and Serving

So often I use fishing as an opportunity for solitude, reflection and recharging. Therefore, I can't say that I have served others extensively through the sport of fishing. Occasionally, however, I have taken a young person fishing so that they can have an opportunity to spend some time outdoors. A fishing trip can provide a chance for a young person to connect with an older person in a unique way, much as I connected with my Uncle Virgil back during World War II. I'm sure that Virgil had other things to do, but his investment in me provided an island of security for me during a time when the world seemed to be coming apart.

I have had opportunities to take the young man I am now mentoring fishing, and this has certainly led to a higher level of mutual understanding. Young people today are growing up in a technology-driven world fueled by computers, video games, cell phones and iPods. They have little contact with nature, and this concerns me greatly.

Sometimes, fishing trips can fail to live up to expectations. Not long after Bo Pelini and his family moved to Lincoln in the winter of 2008, I heard that Bo's son Patrick loved to fish. I asked Patrick if he would like to try ice fishing, and he said he would. I told him to dress warmly as it would be cold, but that it would be worth it as we would catch plenty of fish.

Now, Patrick had recently moved to Nebraska from Louisiana. The day was unusually cold and the wind was blowing, so the windchill was below zero. Patrick was game and hung with it as long as he could, but eventually he acknowledged that his hands were freezing (mine were too). I don't think Patrick was very impressed with my skills as a fishing guide. Hopefully he will give me another chance—the next time will be in the summer, however.

Peace of Mind

It is not always obvious at first glance how to best serve others, and trying to make those moment-by-moment decisions can be stressful. My early-morning routine has long been helpful to me in this regard.

When I was coaching, I woke up at 5:30 A.M. each day to spend 45 minutes or so in prayer and meditation. After getting ready for the day, I arrived at work by 7:00, where I gathered with the rest of the coaching staff for a short time of devotion. One of the coaches would read a verse of Scripture, talk about how that passage had impacted his life and suggest ways that it might affect our team, and then we closed in prayer. The devotional time usually only lasted about 10 minutes or so and was not a requirement for anyone on staff, but nearly everyone attended each and every day. It didn't seem to matter whether or not every person was a believer—the time of spiritual focus, regardless of each person's beliefs, seemed to get everyone off on the right foot.

Another thing that has been helpful in my quest for peace of mind in the midst of turbulent times is the example of John Wooden. Early in my coaching career, I read one of Coach Wooden's books, in which he quoted Cervantes: "The journey is better than the inn." For Coach Wooden, this meant that the process took precedence over the end result—and he lived and coached with this in mind. He started each new season by showing his UCLA basketball players how to properly put on their socks to avoid getting blisters. He focused on the fundamentals of dribbling, passing and shooting, and his practices emphasized running drills with speed and intensity. His definition of "success" is "peace of mind which is a direct result of self-satisfaction in knowing you did your best to become the best that you are capable of becoming."[5] Wooden believed that if his players were diligent in preparing to play their very best, the final score would take care of itself.

John Wooden has had a powerful influence on my life. His focus on the process rather than the final score, his never mentioning the word "winning" to his players, spoke volumes to me as a young coach. I began to worry less about outcomes and focused more on diligent preparation, an adherence to principle rather than the opinion of others, and relationships rather than material rewards. Shifting my focus early in my career to the process, the journey, rather than the final score, was very freeing. I cannot control the end results; they are entirely out of my hands. I can, however, work hard and serve the best way I know how—and the peace of mind that comes with preparation and diligent service is success enough.

Our culture is increasingly obsessed with the bottom line, with the final score. The great temptation when results are the focus, unfortunately, is to cut corners. We see this in business, in politics, in sports and in relationships—ethics, principles, values and character are the first things to go when the bottom line is the only line that matters. In athletics, the mindset of "if we can't beat them, we had better join them" was often the response to schools that were cheating. In the corporate world, the pressure to beat earnings estimates and increase the stock price every 90 days often results in short-term unethical behavior. Enron reported projected future earnings as actual current earnings; this practice boosted the stock price but eventually led to an implosion of the company.

When we focus on the journey, on the other hand, we realize that the *way* we do things matters more than the profit margin, the vote tally, the scoreboard or who "won" the fight about the kids. And when we do things the right way—with honesty, integrity, generosity and respect for others—we experience the peace of mind that is the true hallmark of success.

There was a person in the athletic department here at Nebraska many years ago who was a nice man and did his job well. But it seems like every time I spoke with him, he couldn't stop talking about his retirement. He was doing his job, which he was good at but didn't enjoy very much, to pay for his retirement—and it was going to be great! He had all these plans for everything he was going to do after he retired, all the places he would visit. He was living his life for retirement.

After this man retired, his health went downhill extremely fast and he never got to do all the things he had planned. It was very sad, not just because he died somewhat prematurely, but because he had lived his entire life as a prelude to a retirement "paradise" that never materialized.

Like many football fans around the country, I have been watching the drama between Bobby Bowden and Joe Paterno play out. Both of these men have been coaching for an exceptionally long time and are deadlocked in the race for the all-time most wins in college football. The question many people have is why they are still coaching into their late 70s and early 80s. If, as some suspect, they are focused on being the all-time winningest coach, this goal may not be in the best interest of their fans and players. However, knowing both of them as I do, my guess is that they are still coaching because they enjoy it. They like the challenge, and they appreciate the association they have with their players. Both of them have good coordinators to handle the *X*s and *O*s, are good recruiters, and are excellent leaders and managers of their teams. I suspect that the journey is the most important thing for them and that they have a hard time envisioning themselves doing anything other than coaching.

I remember Bear Bryant as he neared the age of 70, which at the time was about as long as any major college coach had ever coached the game, telling me that when he quit coaching, he would probably "croak." It wasn't long before he did leave coaching, just past his seventieth birthday, and within a few months he indeed did pass away. The official cause of his death was a massive heart attack; however, I would imagine that the stresses involved in leaving something he did so well for a long period of time and that he enjoyed very much may have been a major contributor to his fatal heart attack.

That brings me to my current situation. As many Nebraska fans know, I was named the Interim Athletic Director in October 2007. I was given that title so that I could provide some stability to the athletic department for an undetermined, but relatively brief, period of time. Not long after taking the job, I talked to Chancellor Perlman my concerns that the term "interim" made it somewhat difficult for me to make the moves I felt were necessary for the long-term stability of the athletic department. He removed the title, and I was given a date-certain when I would leave the position after the search had occurred for a new athletic director. The time specified was June 2010.

More recently, the chancellor and I visited and I told him that I had no problem with leaving in June 2010, or earlier for that matter, but that having a departure date etched in stone would result in a great deal of speculation on the part of fans and media over the next year as to who was next in line, who should be interviewed and what direction the department should take under the new athletic director. I felt that this would be a distraction for players, coaches and fans and would not serve the program well. As a result, we took the date-certain out of the equation, and I will stay for an unspecified period of time. The chancellor and I will each evaluate the situation annually. If at any time he feels that it is time for me to go, I will step aside, or if I feel that I can no longer serve the athletic department as well as a new person could, I will leave.

I enjoy what I am doing, but I'm certainly not in it for money or ego gratification. Also, there are some things that Nancy and want to do before we kick the bucket. At the present time, I feel that I can make a contribution to the football program. I can help our programs in recruiting and can offer some sense of stability and permanence. I am also quite interested in making sure that our men's and women's basketball teams have adequate facilities, which will help them to be competitive on a national basis. We have a number of sports that are functioning quite well and could do as well without me as with me. So, there will come a time when I will leave. That day holds no special concern for me, as I know my fundamental mission—serving and honoring God—can be accomplished in other settings. I want to be faithful to that mission right until the end.

We do not know when our lives will come to a close. It might be years from now after a long illness that gives us a chance to tie up loose ends and let everyone important in our lives know how much they are loved. Or it might be sooner than we think. Remember Brook Berringer. We can't control the end results, but we can invest in service, in good work and in relationships while we're here.

Certainly, aging will have an effect on what we can and can't accomplish along the way—I, of all people, know that. As health and energy decline, we may not be able to cover as many miles in a day as we used to, but that doesn't mean we have to stop walking! John Wooden, one of my heroes, is in his 90s, and still personally signs books for fans and admirers who have been inspired and motivated by his legacy. Moses was reportedly 80 when he led the Exodus from Egypt. Winston Churchill's greatest contributions came late in his life. As people live longer and enjoy better health, many are beginning second and third careers.

Having said that, it is extremely important that one does not hang on too long. It is very sad to see someone whose skills and energy have declined continue to occupy a position long after their usefulness has departed. Part of the reason I left coaching was because the way I wanted to coach was very high-energy and I could sense that I could not continue to do that much longer. I hope that I will have the judgment to know when it is time to leave the Athletic Director position.

I don't know what the future holds for me—I can't know, just as I couldn't know on January 2, 1984, that people would still argue 25 years later in sports bars and living rooms across the country about my decision to go for two against Miami. All I can do is take one day at a time, focusing on the journey and on serving the people around me along the way. The end results, I leave in God's hands.

It is my prayer that, in whatever roles you are called to play on the journey of your life, you will experience the peace of mind that comes with knowing you've done your best, no matter the final score. As good as playing and coaching football is, I have discovered there truly is much more to life beyond the game.

Notes

1. ESPN Page 2, "Readers: Best College Football Team," ESPN.com © 2007. http://espn.go.com/page2/s/list/readers/bestCollegefb.html (accessed May 2008).
2. Mark A. Miller, "The Nebraska Song," © 1997 Travelin' Zoo Music, Nashville, TN.
3. Quoted in John Wooden and Jay Carty, *Coach Wooden's Pyramid of Success: Building Blocks for a Better Life* (Ventura, CA: Regal, 2005), pp. 149-150.
4. Nancy Nicosia, Rosalie Liccardo Pacula, Beau Kilmer, Russell Lundberg and James Chiesa, "The Economic Cost of Methamphetamine Use in the United States, 2005," © 2009, The RAND Corporation, Summary p. xiii. www.rand.org/pubs/monographs/2009/RAND_MG829.sum.pdf (accessed June 2009).
5. John Wooden and Jay Carty, *Coach Wooden's Pyramid of Success*, p. 17.

TOM OSBORNE CAREER CAPSULE

Personal Information

Date of Birth: February 23, 1937

Family: Wife, Nancy; Son, Mike; Daughters, Ann and Suzanne

Administrative Experience

Nebraska, Athletic Director, 2007-present

U.S. Congress, Third District (Nebraska), 2000-2006

Nebraska, Head Football Coach, 1973-1997

Nebraska, Assistant Head Football Coach, 1972

Nebraska, Assistant Football Coach, 1967-1971

Educational Ledger

Nebraska, Ph.D. in Educational Psychology, 1965

Nebraska, M.A. in Educational Psychology, 1963

Hastings College, B.A. in History, 1959

Tom Osborne's Honors and Accomplishments

Nebraska Athletic Director, 2007-present

U.S. Congressman (Nebraska's Third District), Three Terms

College Football Hall of Fame Inductee, 1999

Three National Titles, 1994, 1995 and 1997

University of Nebraska Head Coach, 1973-1997

Tom Osborne's Coaching Record

Year	Won	Lost	Tied	Pct.	Bowl	Highlights
1973	9	2	1	.792	Cotton	
1974	9	3	0	.750	Sugar	
1975	10	2	0	.833	Fiesta	Big Eight co-champions
1976	9	3	1	.731	Bluebonnet	
1977	9	3	0	.750	Liberty	
1978	9	3	0	.750	Orange	Big Eight co-champions
1979	10	2	0	.833	Cotton	
1980	10	2	0	.833	Sun	
1981	9	3	0	.750	Orange	Big Eight champions
1982	12	1	0	.923	Orange	Big Eight champions
1983	12	1	0	.923	Orange	Big Eight champions
1984	10	2	0	.833	Sugar	Big Eight co-champions
1985	9	3	0	.750	Fiesta	
1986	10	2	0	.833	Sugar	
1987	10	2	0	.833	Fiesta	
1988	11	2	0	.846	Orange	Big Eight champions
1989	10	2	0	.833	Fiesta	
1990	9	3	0	.750	Citrus	
1991	9	2	1	.792	Orange	Big Eight co-champions
1992	9	3	0	.750	Orange	Big Eight champions
1993	11	1	0	.917	Orange	Big Eight champions
1994	13	0	0	1.000	Orange	National champions
1995	12	0	0	1.000	Fiesta	National champions
1996	11	2	0	.846	Orange	Big 12 North champions
1997	13	0	0	1.000	Orange	National champions
Totals	255	49	3	.836	25 straight	13 conference titles
Bowls	12	13	0	.480	3 national titles	

THANKS

To write a book, especially a memoir, takes a team. I could not have done this without the help of many others who contributed their expertise, time and hard work. I want to say thank you to:

My wife, Nancy, who stood with me as we lived out the moments recorded in this book, sacrificed much and gave of her time to help review the manuscript, even during one of my fishing trips!

To Erin Duncan, my son, Michael, and my daughter Suzanne for diligently reviewing this book to make sure all the facts were recorded correctly.

To my assistants, Anne Hackbart and Sandy McLaughlin, who exemplify an attitude of excellence and putting others first.

To Jonathan Clements, who dreamed up this project.

To the team at Regal Books who have carried out this vision, particularly Regal president Bill Greig III, cover designer Rob Williams, managing editor, Mark Weising, and editors Aly Hawkins, Steven Lawson and Alanna Swanson.

A portion of the proceeds from this book will go to TeamMates to help equip a new generation of leaders and to the University of Nebraska Athletics Student Life Center. If you would like to donate money to either organization, or to learn more information, contact:

TeamMates Mentoring Program
6801 O Street
Lincoln, Nebraska 68510
www.teammates.org

Nebraska Athletics Development Office
One Memorial Stadium
Lincoln, Nebraska 68588-0154
www.huskers.com

To find out more about booking Tom Osborne at your next event, contact:

Jonathan Clements
The Nashville Agency
P.O. Box 110909
Nashville, Tennessee 37222
info@thenashvilleagency.com

To obtain Nebraska football and Tom Osborne videos and memorabilia, log on to:

www.bestofbigred.com